the happy music play book

With my love, and gratitude for your valuable input —
C xx

cordelia williams

Copyright © 2021 by Cordelia Williams

All rights reserved.

Published by Arc Books & Publishing.

Hardback ISBN 978-1-3999-0031-7

No part of this book may be reproduced in any form or by any electronic or mechanical means, including information storage and retrieval systems, without written permission from the author, except for the use of brief quotations in a book review.

www.happymusicplaybook.com

For my mother

Contents

Introduction   **7**
Why I wrote this book and what
you and your child will get from it

1 Why play with music?   **13**

2 Joy, creativity and the 'magic spark'   **19**

3 Encouraging without pushing   **23**
How to nurture creativity

4 Secret musical skills   **27**
What exactly makes a musician?

5 Useful household kit   **31**
Everything you'll need for enjoying music as a family

The Happy Music Play Book

THE GAMES

6 Top ten for babies — 39

7 Adapting your daily routine — 47
Everyday songs and musical habits to keep you
and your child happy, relaxed and entertained

8 Morning rhythm and wriggles — 65
Energetic musical experiments for fizzing whizzbees

9 Top ten under-a-minute — 79

10 Rescue kit for grump emergencies — 89
Turn the day around

11 Rescue kit for exhausted parents — 107
Quiet activities for when you
need a sit down and a cup of tea

12 Breath and movement for mini-musicians — 125
Calm and comfort, discover the body,
help them to b-r-e-a-t-h-e

13 Musical mealtimes — 139
Kitchen dancing and conversation-
starters to fuel the imagination

14 Baths and cuddles — 153
Relaxing sound games and explorations

Contents

15 Favourite music-based books   167
Brilliant children's books featuring music and musicians

16 "Can I have a song?"   173
Bedtime lullabies, the most important part of our day

Glossary   187
Musical words for little kids (and their parents)

Resources and further reading   191
Relevant research and interesting books

Acknowledgements   197

Introduction
Why I wrote this book and what you and your child will get from it

When people find out that my career is playing the piano, they always want to know whether I've already started teaching my two boys. I can sense surprise when I tell them I haven't 'taught' my firstborn anything yet (he's four) and, what's more, I have absolutely no desire to teach him, or his little brother!

Naturally, since I've spent most of my days on earth playing the piano, I can't imagine my children living a life without music. To me, it's a vital joy – playing and hearing music gives my life greater emotional depth and connection and brings inexpressible beauty, excitement, fun and comfort. I hope with all my heart that they'll make music a part of their lives. However, I want it to be something they discover for themselves, with free will, determination and anticipation: a learning experience not so different from mud-splatting, tree-climbing or baking.

Like many parents, I do want to help my children to engage actively with music, to prepare the way for more structured learning later if they're interested. But even more than this, I want to avoid putting any pressure on them to play an instrument. What I'd really like is to enjoy relaxed, happy time together, while somehow also naturally inspiring a love of music. That's not asking too much, is it??

Before I had my first son, I had no idea how I would meaningfully incorporate music into his life without teaching him anything. I knew about toddler music groups, nursery rhymes, and playing peaceful music to help him sleep; although these are all enjoyable, I felt there must be a more creative and personal introduction to music's depth and variety. However, I also wanted to avoid imposing instructions and theory on small children. I felt stuck in a quandary between wanting music to be fun and free from expectation, but at the same time stimulating and challenging. I had no idea how or whether these two things could ever actually coexist.

After four years of cutting my working time down drastically to raise my children, I'm relieved to find that not only do I relish *any* opportunity to engage in music; I've also got into the habit of inventing musical games and sillinesses whenever they pop into my piano-starved, sleep-deprived, caffeine-fuelled brain. I'm writing this book because I want to share with you the ways I've found to make music part of the everyday fabric of your life as a family. This is music *without* teaching: just using the time you have at home together during your child's early years to have fun, rather than treating it as a specific 'activity' that you feel you have to do to make your child more talented or brainy. And because it's easy and fun for *both* of you, it's more likely to generate a positive and lasting relationship with music, something that feels integral to your child's character and experience of life, something they won't rebel against or just forget about as soon as they hit puberty.

The holy grail of music in early childhood is to avoid telling little kids *how* to play at all. We're their parents and playmates, not their teachers. We can share music with them as equals, have fun together, cuddle and laugh at silly songs. We can let them explore the feel of the piano keys or the arrangement of the guitar strings, listen to the sounds around them, experiment with singing, and gradually start learning, instinctively, by themselves. Here are ideas and inspiration for doing just that.

Introduction

This book is a culmination of my experiences as both a professional musician and a parent. Everything I write is informed by my three-decade journey towards a more joyful, spontaneous and physically pleasurable way of performing – the musical equivalent of wiggling my toes in the fresh cool grass. Time and again, the most important thing I've learnt is that the best music, at any level, is play.

I want to reassure and encourage you that you can share music with your family, little by little, to a truly life-changing extent. No matter how unqualified you may feel right now, you have the ability to give them:

- ♫ a joyful relationship with music;
- ♫ an early discovery of their own creativity and imagination;
- ♫ opportunities every day to build confidence and individual thought;
- ♫ the potential to go on and play an instrument (if they want to) with a sense of ease and natural musicianship.
- ♫ music for their souls, not just for the grades.

The foundations of all this are laid during the first years of life, at home with you. You can do it through play, and you can have proper fun doing it.

I also hope that this book will help *you*, as a parent. As a mother, what I've often most wanted and needed are easy ways to engage and entertain my little whirlwinds without becoming utterly exhausted myself. It's mentally draining to think of endless activities for small children, whether you're with them all day every day or for a few hours. This book is a collection of all the little musical ideas I've come up with to pass the days at home, to make my two boys laugh, to calm and comfort, to persuade them to get up the stairs or put on their pants, and sometimes just to amuse myself. I'll give you ways to slip in a little bit of singing or rhythm to the daily routine, and some suggestions (tried and tested on my own little audience of two) which you can turn to when your brain is fried and you just can't think of a single thing to do.

There is a variety of suggestions here, ranging from under-a-minute musical tricks, to short games and experiments, to activities you could spend half an hour doing together. Some of them are more a 'way of being' with your child, of interacting through music while going about your day. I hope that, whatever your personality and musical preferences, and whether you are at home full time, part time or rushing home from work for bedtime, you will find something here to suit your life and to enjoy with your child, which can bring a smile to your day and theirs. You can smile a little extra knowing that each time you sing, play or bash, you are setting your child up for a lifetime of creativity and confidence.

All the songs in this book, plus other resources, can be found arranged by chapter at **www.happymusicplaybook.com** – look out for the ◉ symbol with the appropriate track number each time.

A guide to the musical skills icons can be found in Chapter 4, pp25–27.

About the author

Hearing her mother teach the piano, Cordelia Williams wanted to learn to play too, and began lessons as soon as she could climb onto the piano stool. She received Distinction at Grade 1 aged 4 and gave her first public piano recital to celebrate her eighth birthday. She spent seven years at Chethams School of Music, going on to study at Cambridge University and Guildhall School of Music and Drama, and was BBC Young Pianist of the Year in 2006.

Since then, she has become recognised for the poetry, conviction and depth of her playing. 'Commanding and sensitive' (Sunday Times), she has performed all over the world, including concertos with the English Chamber Orchestra (in Mexico City), City of Birmingham Symphony Orchestra and Royal Philharmonic Orchestra (at Barbican Hall, London), as well as recitals at Wigmore Hall, Royal Festival Hall and Beijing Concert Hall. She has released four critically acclaimed albums.

Cordelia welcomed her first son in 2017, who has accompanied her on several concert tours and was recently joined by a brother. This is her first book.

cordeliawilliams.net

youtube.com/CordeliaWilliams

The Happy Music Play Book

1 Why play with music?

If you'd like to learn more about anything in this chapter, I've provided a 'further reading' list at the back of the book, where you can find all studies and research quoted in the book, plus other relevant writings you may be interested in.

Children are programmed to love music, sound and rhythm. When your baby hears your voice in the womb (from the second trimester), they are learning to distinguish pitches. Hearing is their most developed sense at birth (day-old babies have been shown to discriminate between different rhythmic patterns), and parents naturally make the most of this aural communication by talking in 'parentese' – that melodic, repetitive speech we instinctively use with small babies.

Even if you think you are tone-deaf, I can guarantee that you have already started contributing to your child's musical development simply through your interactions with them since they were born.

There's a lot of research to show that very young babies love the sound of their parents' singing (most of the studies involve mothers but there is also a measurable effect when fathers sing). They respond more raptly to singing than to speaking – in fact, this is probably linked with the development of parentese. Singing calms their heart rate, lowers cortisol levels and results in a reduction in movement; all signs of relaxation. Mothers who sing to their babies also report lower stress levels and an increased sense of bonding: points all round. [1]

In the immediate term, then, it's great to play with music because babies and children love it and it comes naturally to them. They have an instinct for expressing themselves through sound and wriggling their little bodies in response to music. Hearing and making it is exciting for them, it's a fun way for families to spend time together and it provides a mutually enjoyable activity for parents and kids to bond over. I almost feel that those are good enough reasons by themselves for writing this book.

---

[1] Please see 'Resources'.

1: Why play with music?

In the longer term, there are lots of benefits, developmentally and academically. Musical education increases IQ, an effect sustained into adulthood even if music lessons are not continued. Engaging in music also improves children's reading and speech; a study by the University of Queensland showed that informal musical play at home has even stronger benefits than shared reading.[2] Parents of 3,000 children were asked to replace all shared-reading activities with music activities when the children were between two and three years old. Two years later a range of tests showed that shared music was linked with higher social skills, numeracy and concentration.

However, as a parent I'm more interested in how music can give my children a happy, fulfilled life than in how it can make them more successful or intelligent. So, for me, playing and listening to music (of any genre) are inspiring and joyful ways to spend time, to unwind, to socialise and to process or express emotions – and this continues from childhood through to the teenage, student and adult years. Studies have shown that playing music influences long-term well-being, promoting self-esteem and independence, and decreasing anxiety, depression, fatigue and feelings of isolation.

While giving you fun ideas to share together in the here and now may be my first aim, my second is laying the ground for our children to enjoy a musical life in whatever way suits them. When considering music lessons for their children, most parents aren't focused on raising a prodigy or training them to perform as soon as possible. Generally, they want to slowly build up traits and experiences that will foster a lifelong love of music, so that playing and listening to music will remain a comfort and a pleasure to their children through school, university, jobs and families. (Music for life, not just for scholarships.)

The most common path in teaching a child music is to wait until they're old enough, usually between five and ten years old, a) to read music and b) to concentrate in formal lessons of thirty minutes to an hour. Weekly lessons are then supported by daily practice at home.

---

[2] Please see *'Resources'*.

15

The first problem with this method is that, as all parents know, it's pretty hard to force your child to learn anything, let alone to make them enjoy it. If a child's first meaningful experience of music is one where they have to focus on learning scales, patterns on a page, and technique, and then to 'practise' when they're already exhausted after school, it's no surprise so many of our children give up (and regret it later). For many children, this traditional approach simply doesn't allow them to form a genuine connection with the act of making personal, joyful music. Music isn't fun, they can't see the point of it, and therefore it becomes a struggle for them, their teacher and their parents.

Therefore, the first thing we must do is make music fun, free and relaxed, long before lessons and practice enter the equation. Of course there are children (myself included) who adapt well to the formal style of music training, but even these little students will benefit hugely from a joyful, free aspect to their music-making. And, more importantly, what about all those children who need a different approach in order to connect with music? Musical enjoyment and achievement should not be limited to a small subsection of children.

The second problem is that, by the time a child is old enough to read music and concentrate on lessons and practice, their best window for making musical connections has already elapsed. During the earliest years of life the brain is particularly sensitive to different sounds and able to distinguish and remember them, which is why it's so much easier to learn a language as a child (studies show that this aural sensitivity gradually decreases from babyhood and then drops off significantly around the age of six). All babies are born with the potential to learn any language, including music, easily, but during the first years of life the brain quickly starts to prune those synaptic connections which it perceives are not needed. A young child can distinguish the pitch accent of a tonal language like Mandarin Chinese but, if not used, the ability will be gradually lost; it is very difficult for a non-Mandarin-speaking adult to hear and reproduce those inflections accurately. In the

1: Why play with music?

same way, it is much easier for children to pick up a natural, effortless musicality during that golden window of opportunity in early childhood.[3] Therefore, wouldn't it be great to integrate music-making meaningfully into baby- and toddler-hood, before a child wants to take formal instrumental lessons?

My solution to the above two problems is to introduce music gradually through play during the precious pre-school years, in order to give children a relaxed and happy initial relationship with music-making. We can nourish a wonderful all-round musicianship and love of music before they even think about proper instrumental lessons or note-reading. Picking up an instrument later on will simply be a case of channelling their instincts through a certain set of physical actions. From a teacher's point of view, this general musicianship is what makes certain children incredibly easy and rewarding to teach (which leads to more engaging and satisfying lessons for the child, too).

The other main benefit of the playful approach is that it leaves the door open for children to build a passion for music organically and run with it as they get older, under their own steam. This is surely the healthiest, most natural way to learn! It would be so sad to find that the sense of adventure or excitement that music may once have held for a child had been squashed out by overly pressurised 'training' when they weren't ready for it. Let's explore this idea more in Chapters 2 and 3.

---

[3] Please see '*Resources*'.

2 Joy, creativity and the 'magic spark'

This book is full of silly, carefree moments, but behind all that there is something important. At the core of this 'playing with music' approach lies the development of:

- ♪ joy in making music
- ♪ a feeling of creative freedom.

Before developing any specific musical skills or ability, I believe that these are the most essential ingredients for a happy musician, whether simply noodling around at home or performing solos worldwide. Even if your child decides not to continue with an instrument, these gifts will never lose their value.

Joy

More importantly than any particular learning, most of my games are intended to make everyone laugh and to delight in sound and silliness, because we all want our children's lives to be filled with joy, wonder and discovery. This is mainly how I use music with my boys, and music can really help to boost the jolliness levels of everyday life. I also hope that the sense of freedom and possibility they adopt through musical play may even boost their happiness as adults.

In a more practical, forward-looking sense, if your child goes on to learn an instrument (or take up any creative hobby) then the positive associations made by laughing, singing and exploring with you are going to be more effective motivation than a practice star chart or potential music scholarship. If they see music as a pleasurable activity, they're more likely to continue to work at it. It will also be easier to do so: when relaxed and happy, we absorb new experiences and sensory feedback more effectively.

By giving your kids this playful, happy grounding in sound and song, you are also helping them to make music for the innate fun of it, not for a purpose. This is vital if they want to continue with music seriously; some burnt-out child prodigies find, after years of drilling, that they don't actually like playing after all. Without joy and a simple love of the music, there will always be something missing from any performance. This is the case whatever the level of skill – the simplest piece of music can be incredibly moving when overflowing with happiness and enthusiasm. Likewise, no matter how virtuosic or dedicated a musician is, the performance will feel empty without that basic musical joy. So, if your child does end up playing music in any capacity, it's the physical pleasure and exhilaration of producing wonderful sounds that make it a memorable experience, for them and for their audience.

But in any path of life, an enjoyment of playing - of exploring for its own sake - is such a precious attribute. Have a look at 'Chapter 3: Encouraging without pushing' for more on this.

Creativity

'Creativity' simply means the ability to make something new using original ideas. In musical terms, creativity is what will allow a child to produce something that feels personal and unique – expressing something about themselves, or about life, through sound. This can be in writing their own songs or music or, later, in discovering and communicating meaning in the pieces they play.

2: Joy, creativity and the 'magic spark'

Creative, individual thought is an important factor in a successful life, especially for little children growing up in the ever-changing economy of the 21st century. Innovation and adaptability will be key, whatever industry they work in, so creativity is one of the most valuable, rewarding skills we can nurture in our children. (According to LinkedIn, creativity is consistently the soft skill most desired by employers.)

This book is chock-full of opportunities to try out very gradually what it means to create something new and to observe the result. There are games for making new tunes and rhythms, games for using language creatively and games for musical imaginative play. There are also lots of ideas for helping kids to express and develop their individual perceptions and view of the world – that is, to find their creative voice. In each game the outcome is irrelevant – there is no right or wrong answer, so a small child's contribution is just as valuable as a professional musician's. The only goal is to hear and respect what this little person has to say. Children gain so much confidence in their own voice from seeing that you are entertained by, or interested in, what they play or sing. They start to learn that their own creative ideas have value.

The 'magic spark'

In my view, the term 'performance' refers to the wonderful ability to convince and draw in one's audience – you might call it 'magic', '*je ne sais quoi*', or 'the extra bit that can't be taught'. We may not be able to *teach* it exactly, but we can certainly provide the conditions for it to flourish over time.

Joy and creativity, as we've already discussed above, are central to the strange alchemy which gives some children that musical spark. There are other contributing factors, though. True performance is about communicating something that feels real – perhaps an idea, an emotion, a character, an image or a story. The performer and audience feel personally involved with what's being created, and are emotionally invested in the outcome. This is the core of any performing art: dance, theatre, mime, illusion, circus or comedy. What's more, it's a beautiful thing to experience and a skill that translates into different walks of life.

We want to provide the conditions for this magic to start happening. Therefore, areas we most want to nourish through our musical play are:

- ♪ an understanding of music's potential for communication
- ♪ awareness of the emotions
- ♪ self-expression through music
- ♪ awareness of the body
- ♪ comfort with using movement expressively (leading to a natural command of the voice, body or instrument)
- ♪ independence of thought
- ♪ imagination
- ♪ the ability to become absorbed in a creative pursuit.

(This is often known as being in a state of 'flow' or 'being in the zone', which means being so fully absorbed that you lose track of time. Your happiness levels are similarly intensified, and this has been linked with the development of emotional intelligence. See 'Resources' for more information.)

That short list is at the heart of this book. The games and experiments may seem simple, but everything is underpinned by the aims of imagination and communication.

3 Encouraging without pushing

Encouraging your child's interests, hobbies and pursuits without accidentally putting pressure on them to do those things more, or better, is one of the trickiest aspects of parenthood. It's so easy to make a child feel that they have to do well at something in order to please their parents, or even (in extreme cases) in order to be worthwhile and lovable, rather than for the enjoyment and challenge of doing the thing itself. This external locus of reward or 'extrinsic motivation', which requires constant praise and recognition, is not a helpful mindset to carry through life, as it undermines the idea that an activity has its own inherent value or interest. (If you wish to read more about extrinsic and intrinsic motivation, please see 'Resources'.) Children naturally enjoy learning about their world and all we need to do is avoid getting in the way of that.

In trying to give my boys a long-term, healthy relationship with music and learning, I always come back to two main principles:

- ♪ provide lots of opportunities
- ♪ allow space for independent learning.

I follow these principles as much as possible and they're as close as you'll get to guidelines in this book.

Opportunity

I believe that every child is born with music in their bones. The ones who end up being obviously 'musical' are those who were exposed to music from an early age and were thus able to adopt it easily as a kind of mother-tongue. In the same way as learning to talk, a mastery of music comes with the many little opportunities to communicate and experiment each day. (Of course, personality and circumstance also have an effect on future musical talent, but in general they won't replace the ease of musical communication gained from early exposure to music.)

As parents, we can help our children develop a love and an ear for music by providing them with regular and consistent exposure to the building blocks of music. Hearing a variety of sounds, melodies and rhythms in an unforced and relaxed home setting will allow them to absorb the multitude of musical possibilities. Given time, they will start experimenting and making music their own, just like picking up new words each day and gradually starting to form their own quirky sentences.

The ideas in this book will help you make as many tiny opportunities as possible for your child to hear and engage with music each day, ideally in a variety of ways. Your little explorers will quickly start to understand how sounds can fit together to make music, without even realising that they're learning. If and when they do choose an instrument later, they'll be steeped in music from the inside out, and the instrument will feel like an extension of something that is already a natural form of communication for them.

Space

When babies take their first steps, we don't instruct them how to place each foot in front of the other. We give them the space to pick it up in their own sweet time, and to find the best way of using their limbs (which, after all, they know better than we do).

3: Encouraging without pushing

Likewise, the key to preserving a child's enthusiasm for an activity is to leave them to learn at their own speed and in their own direction. This way, they feel in control of the endeavour - the voyage of discovery belongs to them. They'll pick things up gradually, refining their skills through experimentation and instinctive adjustment, without any external input from you. But most importantly, they will feel a sense of delight and self-motivation because they have learnt it 'all by myself'. All parents know that as soon as your child notices you interfering or trying to control the outcome, they start to withdraw and lose interest.

Trust in your child's ability to learn by themselves and give them the space to do it. You don't need to teach, just to join in with their fun. If you need to, stick a reminder on your fridge to simply listen and enjoy. It can be very hard for us to step back and watch our children not being good at something – we all automatically want to improve their strategy or technique. But valuing their efforts for what they are (and avoiding the temptation to make constant 'suggestions') will save you both a great deal of frustration. Creativity is difficult to nurture but very easy to destroy!

Learning slow

In his book *Range: How Generalists Triumph in a Specialized World*, David Epstein uses the term 'learning slow', which I find a helpful concept. A holistic, experimental style of learning often means slower initial progress: the student is taking time to a) make connections across a range of experience and knowledge, and b) discover how to learn independently, overcome challenges and deal with frustration. Despite this, 'learning slow' predicts higher performance later in life – it's a long-term approach. Faster initial learning, meanwhile, which may be achievement-based or focused on immediate results and feedback, actually undermines long-term development.

By giving your child the space to learn about music for themselves, you're allowing them this period of free experimentation. You're also helping to develop a healthy sense of internal motivation – they are learning for their own pleasure and for learning's inherent reward, rather than to please you. Finally, you're teaching them to trust in the process of learning through trial and error and to know that you have confidence in them. These things seem so worthwhile – in music of course, but also in the wider context of all education.

I'm going to keep a little motto in the back of my mind throughout my time as a parent: 'Learn slow, enjoy forever'.

4 Secret musical skills
What exactly makes a musician?

In addition to having fun together and passing the day more joyfully, this book will help you to gradually explore the different elements of musicianship in a relaxed and creative way. Your little one will be picking up musical skills and understanding without having any idea that they're learning. Underneath each game or activity, you'll find a small picture from this key if any of these skills is particularly involved.

Pitch

- ♪ How high or low different notes are
- ♪ The relationship between notes
- ♪ Singing in tune
- ♪ The ability to hear, remember and copy a tune

Rhythm

- ♪ Tempo (speed)
- ♪ Pulse (a regular beat)
- ♪ Copying specific rhythmic patterns
- ♪ Not being that person at the party who claps on the wrong beat

Tone

- ♪ Sensitivity to sound qualities, colours and textures (e.g. clarity, richness or harshness)
- ♪ Controlling the sound produced in order to create different effects

Shape

- ♪ Dynamics (loud or soft)
- ♪ Articulation (short or long)
- ♪ Phrasing (e.g. singing a line in one smooth breath, in shorter sections, or in a disjointed way)
- ♪ Understanding why and how music has different characters

Improvisation

♪ Making up music freely and spontaneously

♪ Having fun with sound and going with the flow

♪ Feeling comfortable instead of self-conscious

(Improvisation is so often neglected in musical training, even amongst professional musicians, but having the confidence and open-mindedness to improvise is a priceless skill.)

Listening

♪ Interest in the sounds and music around us

♪ Detailed listening and observation

♪ Interpretation of music's meanings

♪ Building confidence in describing and discussing what the child hears

(This is, of course, a valuable skillset in any educational, professional or social setting.)

Performance

♪ Communication and self-expression

♪ Physical and emotional awareness

♪ Imagination and creativity

(Please refer to Chapter 2, above, for more on 'performance')

5 Useful household kit
Everything you'll need for enjoying music as a family

You don't need to spend lots of money on expensive equipment or instruments to enjoy the activities in this book. Before we get started, here's a list of things you could gather into your main playing area, or an easily accessible place. Some of these you'll have already around the house; some might be a possible next birthday present from the grandparents. But they're all optional – if you only have your voice and a radio (or the internet), you're good to go.

Easy to find around the house:

A shaker. Maracas and tambourines are a few pounds each new, but can also often be found in charity shops. Alternatively, you could make your own by pouring some dried lentils, nuts, or pasta into a plastic bottle (with a *very* tightly fitting lid!). If you have a toddler they could even paint the pasta shapes different colours to make their own special shaker. Small plastic toys in a tin also work.

A drum. We've never had a proper drum, but we use saucepans and boxes. We have some children's drumsticks (less pointy than adult ones) for when the drummers are feeling more precise and hands just won't do. You could also paint some Tupperware boxes to use as drums – different sizes and materials will make different sounds.

Some kind of bell. A wind chime, gong or triangle would provide lots of entertainment and interest, experimenting with sounds. Basic versions can be found for between £2 and £15.

Your recycling bin (see pages 108 and 140)

A radio (see pages 38, 61 and 144)

Despite having all our music accessible online via phones, I have found it immensely useful to have a proper **hi-fi / CD player** with a stack of our favourite CDs next to it. It just seems easier in the heat of the moment to pop in a CD than to search for something appropriate online while a small person tries to grab your phone and eat it. This might just be me though. (See page 90 for more on my emergency CD stack.)

It would be handy to work out your preferred **system for making playlists**, whether on iTunes, Spotify, Youtube or wherever you listen to music. There are a few activities in the book which work well with a playlist, so it's a good investment of time to familiarise yourself with the technology now.

Optional extras:

Any musical instrument you can afford or find. Perhaps a family member has a banjo that's no longer used, or a neighbour may have an old school recorder in the attic.

A child's **xylophone** is wonderful. The metal ones (technically called glockenspiels) make a brighter, clearer sound, while the wooden ones are more mellow. Those with different-coloured bars help little ones distinguish between the notes (see page 57 for the best colour arrangement). I found our wooden one in a charity shop for £5.

5: Useful household kit

Harmonicas and ukuleles are fun, small and cheap (£5-10 and £20 respectively). Both good for little hands.

Guitars — they come in child-friendly sizes as well as full sizes. We also have **home-made guitars:** stretch different sized elastic bands around a box or a pot or pan. The smaller elastic bands will be stretched tighter and will make higher sounds. The quality of any of these instruments doesn't matter — it's just for experimenting (in fact, it's possibly a case of 'the cheaper, the better', since they will undoubtedly become well-loved and a bit bashed around over time).

A piano — if you can get hold of one. Second-hand upright pianos can be very cheap in local listings or charity shops — and eBay has older models for between £10 and £300, or even free, sometimes. A piano is not essential for using this book, but they are lovely things to have in a family home; children gravitate towards pianos and there is something immensely comforting about having an instrument standing there in a corner, waiting to be played. (If you're buying a very old or out-of-shape piano, it might be sensible to factor in the cost of a piano tuner to get it sounding its best again.)

A **keyboard** is also a perfectly good option, and is more portable and practical, especially if you lack space. One with 'weighted keys' (also known as 'touch sensitive') and a pedal attachment is a more long-term purchase, if they go on to play more seriously. I do feel pianos and keyboards are worth the cost in the long run as, unlike other toys, they will last a child for life. You can also get free **'piano keyboard' apps** for phones, tablets or computers, which would be good if you're short on physical space.

The Happy Music Play Book

A pat on the back and a large glass of wine. Whatever you can find of the above, I hope you feel immensely proud to be giving your child happy music-making during their most formative years. As well as getting more fun, more creative days, you can luxuriate in the knowledge that you are investing a few minutes here and there in their future musicianship, imagination, confidence and general life success.

Some last thoughts before we begin...

The whole is greater than the sum of its parts

Many of the ideas in this book are not particularly complex or ingenious. You may already do some of them, which I hope is a comforting and encouraging thought. But, in collecting them all in one place, I want to provide you with a varied 'deck of cards' ready to whip out as and when needed, as ease and regularity really ingrain music in your child's heart.

After each chapter is a blank page where, if you like, you can make a note of any games or activities which worked particularly well for you and your little one(s). These could be useful reminders of tried-and-tested favourites, or a lovely, lasting record of the happy musical times you spent together.

No objective, no pressure

Most of the games I have included in this book aren't the type you would normally schedule - I don't tend to announce 'Now we're going to play this fun game!' There's no specific objective or a correct way of doing any of these – they're all just opportunities for free play between the two (or three, or four, or more!) of you.

So, choose an idea that you'd like to try out, and keep it tucked up your sleeve for when an empty moment presents itself. If your children join in, great; if they listen for a while then go and do something else, that's great, too. And if they're totally uninterested, it really doesn't matter – you haven't spent any time or money on it, so just leave it and try it another time.

Embrace embarrassment

You may need to temporarily lock away your sense of dignity (if you have given birth or gone out with baby sick on your shirt and yesterday's pants in your pocket, you may have this one sorted already). The key to having musical fun with children is a willingness to look a complete fool. Don't worry about what your voice sounds like or about the musical refinement (or otherwise) of your efforts. Just have a go and be thankful that no one will hear except your child, who still thinks you are the best performer in the world.

The Games

6 Top ten for babies

Playing with young babies can sometimes be a challenge, particularly before they're old enough to hold toys or sit up, but you can introduce music into your daily routine even with the youngest newborn. They will love the sounds, the rhythm and, of course, your interaction with them during these special moments.

These were my favourite easy tricks for a more musical day during the first year - tiny opportunities to respond or communicate musically, and ways to explore sound together which might engage or soothe your baby. Including one of these each day, or whenever you think of it, is more than enough, and a wonderfully musical start to any baby's life. Why not pick one that appeals to you and see if you can find a few opportunities to slip it in today?

The Happy Music Play Book

1. Switch the radio on

This may seem absurdly obvious but it's amazing how often with a newborn I would go for days without thinking of the radio, and then suddenly remember how much more welcoming and chilled-out the house is with music in the background. I really do think that babies absorb and respond to music even during the very earliest days – when we listened to something calming like Bach or Mozart, both mine would visibly (and audibly) relax. The radio is a great way for them to hear a wide variety of music, including things that you would never otherwise think of listening to.

2. Baby dancing

While your baby is lying down or in a baby chair, hold their hands or ankles and gently dance their limbs in time with the music. Again, this helps them feel the pulse and the character of the music: gentle movements for calm music, more energetic movements for up-tempo music. They'll also gain more awareness of their body and their various limbs – during the first six months especially it will be quite exciting for them to stretch out their little arms and legs. Tiny bodies get tired easily, though, so a minute or two of gentle movement is great. You could choose soothing or exciting music depending on your baby's mood.

3. The snuggle jiggle

Before babies can move much, being able to engage physically with what they're hearing must be incredibly empowering! So even if it seems too simple for words, dance with your baby whenever you hear music: cuddle them in your arms or in the sling, and sway, bounce and twirl around the room. Your movements will let them feel the rhythm and energy of the music. Apart from anything else, music relaxes us adults and dancing releases endorphins, and you can't have too many endorphins or relaxation in a baby's first year. This works particularly well if your baby is a bit fretful.

4. Rhythm kisses

With music playing in the background, kiss them in time with the pulse. This will get you all sorts of music-based smiles! Alternatively, you could sing them a nursery rhyme, then repeat the song's rhythm again but in kisses instead of singing. They'll enjoy feeling the different rhythms at the same time as getting extra kisses.

5. Musical aeroplanes

Lift them up and down (gently!) with the pitch if you are listening to music or singing – up when the music is higher, down when it's lower. You'll probably get more giggles with this after the first few months, but it is also a fun flying viewpoint for very small babies.

6. 'Rings on her fingers and bells on her toes'

A very easy trick that fascinates smaller babies is to attach little bells to their wrists or ankles. This is a lovely gentle way for them to interact with the world when they're very young and immobile. They'll also start learning about cause and effect, and that they can control events in their world: *"I moved something: it made a noise! It happened again!"* You can get special wrist bells on Velcro, but I just used one of those gold ones on a red ribbon from a Lindt chocolate bunny. (I probably can't officially recommend that… health and safety…) See if they notice where the sound is coming from when you move the bell to a different limb.

7. Calming playlist

Here are my best music suggestions for soothing newborns, with space to add your baby's own favourites:

▶ 01

- ♪ Beethoven: 'Spring' Sonata for violin and piano (recommended recording: Renaud Capuçon & Franck Braley)
- ♪ Barber: Adagio for strings (Marin Alsop & Royal Scottish National Orchestra)
- ♪ Mozart: Piano Concertos (Mitsuko Uchida)
- ♪ Eric Whitacre: Light & Gold album (Eric Whitacre Singers)
- ♪ Bach & Arvo Pärt: Piano Music (Cordelia Williams)
- ♪ Chopin: Nocturnes (Arthur Rubinstein)
- ♪ Bach: St. Matthew Passion (The Monteverdi Choir)
- ♪ Satie: Gymnopédies (Anne Queffélec)

....
....
....
....
....
....
....

8. Noise machine

Let them watch your mouth close up, making all sorts of different sounds. This is great for tiny ones since their favourite toy is your face and they will absolutely love watching it make funny shapes and noises. Raspberries, *vvvvvvvv* sounds, whistling, squeaking, popping sounds, *oooooooo* sounds, clicking your tongue or your teeth – the more types of sounds you can come up with, the more connections they'll make in terms of tonal possibilities.

Once they're a bit older, they'll start copying you, which is amazing to witness! Apart from your mouth, you can use your body and theirs as an instrument – show them what noise comes out when you tap different body parts, click your fingers, clap, or pop your finger out of your cheek.

9. House sounds

Likewise, explore the sounds of household objects. Anything crinkly like tin foil, baking paper or a jiffy bag is perfect (but don't leave them alone or it'll get eaten!); scratchy Velcro; rubbing different types of hairbrush or comb over a hard surface to make swishing noises; scratching your nails on wicker baskets, the carpet or rough hessian rugs; zips pulled at different speeds. Everything can be used to make a noise!

Aside from anything musical, this is a fantastic way to learn about different textures and will keep them amused like nothing else – household objects are much more interesting than actual baby toys, it seems. Banging a variety of saucepans and containers with a wooden spoon will occupy them for hours. Give them the lids too and prepare for total chaos.

10. Babbling echoes

When they start making noises that you can repeat back to them, try one of these musical variations:

♪ Match their pitch as well as the syllable or noise they are making

♪ Turn their noises/syllables into a simple tune of two or three notes, like the start of 'Three Blind Mice' or 'Hot Cross Buns'

♪ Become a baby-beatboxer and make up little rhythmic patterns using their sounds and syllables. For example:

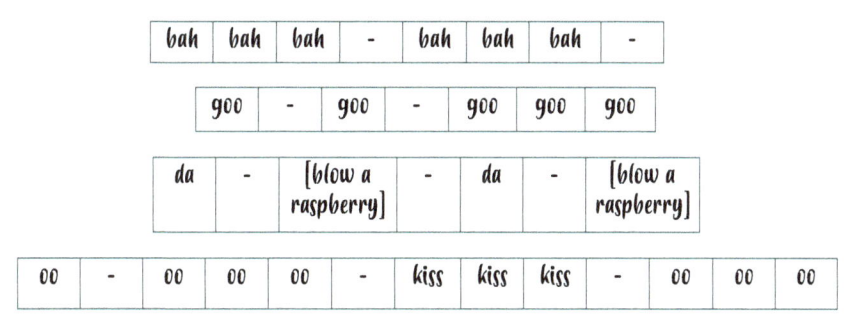

| bah | bah | bah | - | bah | bah | bah | - |

| goo | - | goo | - | goo | goo | goo |

| da | - | [blow a raspberry] | - | da | - | [blow a raspberry] |

| oo | - | oo | oo | oo | - | kiss | kiss | kiss | - | oo | oo | oo |

Repetition is the key here – any repeated pattern becomes a rhythm that they can start to anticipate and enjoy.

You can have quite a varied and entertaining conversation in this way (for both parties). As well as enjoying hearing the different rhythms, babies flourish emotionally with this kind of mirroring, where they do something and see or hear it reflected back at them by a parent. It is so valuable for bonding and for a feeling of security and sense of self. This kind of responsive interaction is wonderful at any stage of childhood, helping a child to feel heard, validated and understood. For more on mirroring, see 'Resources'.

The Happy Music Play Book

Our family's favourite activities: babies

Date　　**Name of game**　　　　　　**Reaction**

……………　……………………………　……………………………………

……………　……………………………　……………………………………

……………　……………………………　……………………………………

……………　……………………………　……………………………………

……………　……………………………　……………………………………

……………　……………………………　……………………………………

……………　……………………………　……………………………………

……………　……………………………　……………………………………

……………　……………………………　……………………………………

……………　……………………………　……………………………………

……………　……………………………　……………………………………

……………　……………………………　……………………………………

……………　……………………………　……………………………………

7 Adapting your daily routine
Everyday songs and musical habits to keep you and your child happy, relaxed and entertained

The previous chapter was all about how to be musical with babies who are limited in their movements. Now we'll find small, easy ways to work music into your everyday life with a child who is becoming an independent little person. Of course, you can still adapt any of these ideas for infants.

I have very little creative brain power left when short of sleep and answering fifteen bizarre questions a minute while also making lunch and trying to stop the baby from falling down the stairs or eating the loo brush. These simple habits give me a break from having to think or make decisions – I just roll out some version of the same old tricks, depending on what's happening at the time, and this generally improves our mood and our interactions. I might do one, two or three of these each day, which means by bedtime we've had a bit of music with pretty much no effort.

Using certain songs for different rituals and transitions through the day gives an extra sense of recognition and predictability to your routine, and most people agree that children thrive on predictability and consistency. In musical terms, activity-based songs start building their awareness of the mood and meaning of a variety of music and make music part of their natural communication. Even better, you might get to sit on the floor for a few minutes singing, instead of chasing someone with their socks or trying to think how dolphins sleep and why sheep are white.

The Happy Music Play Book

7: Adapting your daily routine

Good morning songs

Starting the day with a song puts everyone in a good mood. If you combine it with opening the curtains it will have the extra benefit of reinforcing that precious distinction between sleeping time and awake time. You could choose any uplifting song that makes you feel good, but here are a few weather- and morning-related suggestions to start the day. (You can find these songs at happymusicplaybook.com if you need to remind yourself of the words.)

The Sun Has Got His Hat On (Ambrose & his orchestra) ⊙02

Rain, Rain, Go Away! (traditional) ⊙03

Good Morning! (from Singin' in the Rain) ⊙04

(Possibly modify the lyrics to be more child-appropriate… I sing 'We've slept the whole night through' instead of 'We've talked…', and 'It's great to be awake' instead of '…to stay up late'.)

I Say a Little Prayer (Burt Bacharach) ⊙05

Tomorrow (from Annie) ⊙06

Wake Me Up Before You Go-Go (Wham!) ⊙07

WASHING, RUBBING AND SCRUBBING
Here We Go Round the Mulberry Bush ▶08

is a highly useful song as it can be adapted for absolutely anything you happen to be doing at the time. (Another variant on the same tune is 'Here we go gathering nuts in May'.)

> *Here we go round the mulberry bush,*
> *The mulberry bush, the mulberry bush.*
> *Here we go round the mulberry bush*
> *On a cold and frosty morning.*
>
> *This is the way we wash our face,*
> *Wash our face, wash our face.*
> *This is the way we wash our face*
> *On a cold and frosty morning…*

Other verses can include:

- This is the way we comb our hair
- … wash our hands
- … tie our shoes
- … put on our clothes
- … make the tea
- … tidy the toys
- … scrub the floor etc.

For some reason, singing the song makes doing the action much more fun. This is a good way to engage your toddler if you have a new baby who needs changing, cleaning or dressing. You could also make a game out of your child doing each action for their teddies; they'll enjoy thinking up their own verses.

7: Adapting your daily routine

Tuneful teeth

I made up a specific tooth-brushing song to distract the boys and make them stay still when they only wanted to chew or avoid the toothbrush. It still works on Laurence, three years later. I wouldn't necessarily recommend this as a quality example of lyrical skill, and I'm sure you could find other, better, tooth-related songs to sing. But…

(sung to the tune of 'Mud, Mud, Glorious Mud' / 'Food, Food, Glorious Food')

> *Brush, brush, brushing our teeth,*
> *Nothing quite like it for cleaning the teeth,*
> *So smear on the toothpaste,*
> *And spit out the toothpaste,*
> *And that is the way that we bru-u-ush our teeth.*

(You're welcome.)

Rub a Dub Dub

This rhyme always seems entertaining, whether washing their face, cleaning an object or the house, or drying them after a bath or swimming (I vividly remember squealing with delight while my father power-dried us with a big fluffy towel in time to this rhythm – one of my strongest childhood memories). Everyone seems to have a totally different version of this – you can have a bit of fun making up the silliest possible last line, which will appeal to their sense of the ridiculous.

> *Rub-a-dub-dub,*
> *Three men in a tub,*
> *And who do you think they be?*
> *The butcher, the baker,*
> *The candlestick-maker,*
> *All put out to sea.*

The Happy Music Play Book

OR

Rub-a-dub-dub,
Three men in a tub,
And who do you think they be?
The butcher, the baker,
The candlestick-maker,
Turn 'em out, knaves all three!

OR

Rub-a-dub-dub,
Three men in a tub,
And who do you think were there?
The butcher, the baker,
The candlestick-maker,
And all of them gone to the fair.

OR (my favourite; thanks to Lizzie's mother…)

Rub-a-dub-dub,
Three men in a tub,
And who do you think they be?
The butcher, the baker,
The candlestick-maker,
They all turned into a baked potato!

7: Adapting your daily routine

Climb in time

If someone needs encouraging to get up or down the stairs, for example to get dressed or to leave the house, pick an energetic song and climb in time with the beat. You can loudly drum the beat on the stairs behind them for extra laughter. (For more on marching to a beat, see 'Morning rhythm & wriggles' on page 64)

Try one of these:

Grand Old Duke of York ○09

Oh, the grand old Duke of York,
He had ten thousand men,
He marched them up to the top of the hill,
And he marched them down again.

And when they were up, they were up,
And when they were down, they were down,
And when they were only half-way up,
They were neither up nor down.

Those Magnificent Men and Their Flying Machines ○10

Yankee Doodle ○11

Yankee Doodle went to town
Riding on a pony,
Stuck a feather in his cap
And called it macaroni.

COUNTING AND SORTING

These can be rolled out whenever you are counting anything, cutting their nails, washing hands, using bricks or toys with numbers on them, or absolutely any other activity involving numbers.

Once I Caught a Fish Alive ⊙12

One, two, three, four, five
Once I caught a fish alive
Six, seven, eight, nine, ten
Then I let it go again.

Why did you let him go?
Because he bit my finger so
Which finger did he bite?
This little finger on my right.

See if you can make up a verse for eleven to twenty…

The Ants Go Marching ⊙13

The ants go marching one by one, hurrah, hurrah.
The ants go marching one by one, hurrah, hurrah.
The ants go marching one by one,
The little one stops to suck his thumb.
And they all go marching down,
To the ground, to get out, of the rain.
BOOM! BOOM! BOOM! BOOM!

…two by two… tie her shoe…
…three… climb a tree…
…four… shut the door…
…five… take a dive…
…six… pick up sticks…
…seven… pray to heaven…
…eight… check the gate…
…nine… check the time…
…ten… say "The End!"

7: Adapting your daily routine

Musical tidying timer

I once made up a 'tidying the bricks' song to encourage my very reluctant tidier, but it was even worse than the tooth-brushing song (the only lyrics were 'We're tidying the bricks'). You could make up your own silly one; or, like I now do, pick a jolly song to listen to that lasts the right amount of time for a decent toy tidy (or whatever other chore needs doing). Three minutes seems plenty in my experience. Agree the plan of action with your deputies, count down: "Ready… steady… GO!", press 'Play' and try to get all the bricks in the box before the song ends. Some suggestions are:

'Calling All Workers' ⊙14 or **'Dambusters'** ⊙15 by Eric Coates: both extremely energetic and mood-boosting

'Good Vibrations' ⊙16 by the Beach Boys

Or the classic **'Spoonful of Sugar'** ⊙17 from Mary Poppins herself. "You find the fun and snap! The job's a game."

Baking songs

Baking is a fun activity to do with your little ones, and accompanying it with music makes it even more rewarding. Here are a couple of songs to use if you bake together sometimes – they could be adapted for any cooking-related activity.

Do You Know the Muffin Man? ○18

*Do you know the muffin man,
The muffin man, the muffin man,
Do you know the muffin man,
Who lives on Drury Lane?*

*Yes, I know the muffin man,
The muffin man, the muffin man,
Yes, I know the muffin man,
Who lives on Drury Lane.*

This rhyme refers to English muffins rather than the American cupcake variety; in the past these would have been delivered door-to-door by a muffin man. The best thing about this song is that you can make up verses for all sorts of other ingredients and baked goods. March around the kitchen, taking turns to be the muffin / yogurt / coffee / vegetable man (the idea is that all the children follow the muffin man with his trays of fresh muffins, like the Pied Piper of baked goods). Laurie has now decided that there is a sun-cream man, which proves that the possibilities really are endless.

Hot Cross Buns ○19

*Hot cross buns,
Hot cross buns,
One a penny, Two a penny,
Hot cross buns.*

*If you have no daughters,
Give them to your sons,
One a penny, Two a penny,
Hot cross buns.*

7: Adapting your daily routine

*If your sons don't like them,
They're the only ones,
One a penny, Two a penny,
Hot cross buns.*

*Get them while they're hot
and eat them by the ton,
One a penny, Two a penny,
Hot cross buns.*

Likewise, just change the lyrics to fit with whatever you're baking that day.

The Happy Music Play Book

Loo tunes

We spend a ridiculous amount of time waiting for someone to produce something on the potty or the loo. It's a nice gap to fill with some music.

Get to know the sound of a scale (for anyone who didn't learn scales as a child, this is simply all the notes played in order, either going up or going down. You can play it on a xylophone by starting at the biggest bar and playing each in turn to the smallest one – that's an ascending scale).

- Play the scale, then try singing it and see if they can copy each note in turn.
- Put some words to your scale. I recently found myself singing 'Rafe has done a very good wee' to an ascending scale. (I did question my life choices for a few moments.)
- Let them make up some words – encourage them to use what they see in the bathroom as inspiration ('I can see a tap in the bath').

If they seem to be enjoying this you could, over time, play around with assigning colours of the rainbow to each note (red for lowest, violet for highest). The colours give something more solid to get hold of, to cement the memory of each sound and help to distinguish between pitches. There are accepted colours associated with the notes so these would be the easiest ones to use (most children's xylophones follow this pattern):

7: Adapting your daily routine

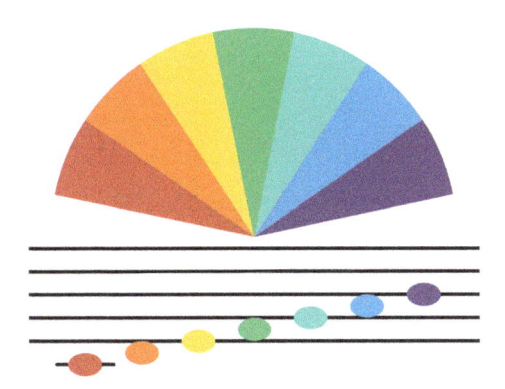

(Note: These colours, as well as matching hand signs, are part of the solfège system. I'll discuss the whole system in 'Resources'.)

Some variations:

- Sing the relevant colour for each note.
- Hold up a coloured brick or card for each note you sing or play on the xylophone.
- One of you names a colour for the other to play or sing the relevant note (takes a bit of practice!)

QUIET MOMENTS
Song building

Fill a few 'I'm bored' minutes during the day by making a song together. For adults, the idea of thinking up a song on the spot can be pretty nerve-wracking, if not downright terrifying. However, children haven't yet developed that self-consciousness or anxiety about doing it well, so you might be surprised by how up for this they are. It doesn't matter if the result doesn't sound much like 'music'; this is only about encouraging them to feel comfortable and free with creating sounds spontaneously.

I use one of two strategies for this.

1. The easy method is to make up some new words for a familiar tune (which we've already introduced quite a bit of), to suit a new occasion or topic of their choosing. Here's another of my masterpieces to start you off, composed while passing a building site:

   (sung to the tune of 'In the Jungle' from The Lion King)
   A-rumble, rumble, rumble, rumble, rumble, rumble, rumble,
   I'm a mixer, a mighty mixer,
   I'm mixing up cement (a-rumble rumble rumble)
   I'm a mixer, a mighty mixer,
   I'm mixing up cement (a-rumble rumble rumble).

   This one was particularly well-received and is often requested, which shows you how basic the requirements are.

7: Adapting your daily routine

Jot down a few topics that you and your child might enjoy building a song about. You could even add any associated words you think of, to keep as possible lyrics. Just in case you need them one day.

....

....

....

....

....

....

....

....

....

....

....

....

....

....

The Happy Music Play Book

2. The other option is simply to see if they'll sing you a song (or play a 'piece' on an instrument) about something that is going on at the time. They may have lots of ideas – if not, help them choose from one of the following categories:

- an exciting event of that day (e.g. seeing a plane or other vehicle, a dog chasing a ball, or a party)
- a person you saw that day
- what have the teddies been doing today?
- a favourite picture or story

Laurence likes making up music for me (I think in return for all the songs I sing him, which is rather sweet) and most of his piano-based efforts feature vehicles crashing into each other or events on a building site. I always comment on some element of how it sounded, before asking seriously "And what was it about?" It's tempting to constantly praise children's abilities in order to encourage them but, since learning about how excessive praise can contribute to a 'fixed mindset', I've tried to focus my observations on what Laurence has done and how he did it, rather than how well he did it. For more on 'fixed' and 'growth' mindsets, see 'Resources'.

My favourite of his so far was *'House song, house song… where the windows are… where the tables are… where the curtains are… house song, house song.'*

Winding down with the radio

As with infants, try getting into the habit of having the radio on during days at home. Even if it's just playing in the background it can provide some nice conversation starters, and (at least in my house) everyone seems happier to get with their own thing while the music and presenters provide company. Any music station will do; we always have BBC Radio 3, except if I'm feeling particularly tired and emotional, in which case Classic FM provides easy, comforting listening.

The Happy Music Play Book

Our family's favourite activities: daily routine

Date   **Name of game**   **Reaction**

8 Morning rhythm and wriggles
Energetic musical experiments for fizzing whizzbees

I find it quite bizarre how children wake up and are immediately playing at 60 mph. If I ever get to full speed these days, it takes at least two cups of tea, a shower and a cup of coffee to reboot my brain. However, my kids don't seem to have got the memo, and the requests to "play with me!" begin regardless of my caffeine status. I marvel at their constant capacity to learn, but I also dread having to think up (and set up) engaging activities of a Tuesday morning, with a semi-functioning brain.

On those (numerous) occasions when I've totally failed to get organised with any kind of activity, craft or 'learning experience', I sometimes use one of these sound-based games to get our day off to a positive start. They involve no setting up or preparation, but allow us to spend a bit of time together (hopefully laying the foundations for some independent play afterwards while I sort out the house and myself) and absorb some of that boundless energy. This chapter combines music with movement and the curiosity that comes so naturally to children. They'll never know they're learning, and you'll wear them out a bit in advance of their lunchtime rest.

The Happy Music Play Book

March in time

Marching to music is good exercise, a fantastic way to develop a strong sense of rhythm and pulse, and will help coordination of body and movements. So that seems like a good place to start. Don't worry if they don't march properly in time at first. They'll pick it up gradually, especially if you join in sometimes and show them where the beat is.

- **Optional:** Find a picture or video of soldiers, guards or a marching band marching, to inspire your troops.

- Pick your marching music (anything with a strong beat). The easiest and most obvious is **The Grand Old Duke of York** (see 51). Alternatively, **Scotland the Brave ◯20**, **The Great Escape ◯21** and the **Thunderbirds theme tune ◯22** are excellent. Or try an online playlist: 'Marching', 'Famous Marching Band Music' or 'Best British Marches'.

- Design a marching route around the house. Take it in turns to lead – make sure the music is loud enough to hear everywhere!

- Perhaps fashion yourselves some tall hats like the guards at Buckingham Palace (an empty cereal box was popular here).

- **Optional:** beat time with a shaker, drum or tambourine (or makeshift equivalent, see page 29) while they march. Then let them beat time while you march, which they will probably find hilarious.

March with your arms

As a variation, once they've vaguely got the hang of marching in time, you could beat with your arms instead of the feet.

- Swing them like pendulums.
- Alternate your arms punching up to the ceiling.
- Punch out to the sides, either together or alternately.
- Straighten them in front of you and clap like seals.

As a bonus, you will get an upper-arm workout.

The shoulders on the bus

Take turns choosing different body parts and thinking what they might do on that famous bus.

> *The wheels on the bus go round and round,*
> *Round and round, round and round,*
> *The wheels on the bus go round and round,*
> *All day long.*

Here are some ideas to get you started:

- The shoulders on the bus scrunch up and down
- The arms on the bus stretch out and in
- The heads on the bus turn left and right
- The ears on the bus lean side to side
- The bottoms on the bus shake all around
- The eyebrows on the bus wiggle up and down.

Simon Says

I'm sure everyone knows this one (by the way, Simon Says works unbelievably well to trick a child into tidying up their own room). But you can also do a musical version.

Quick recap of the rules: one person is 'Simon' and gives instructions to the other players. Instructions should be followed ONLY when prefaced with the phrase "Simon says…". So if you say, "Simon says: march like a soldier", they march. But if you say, "March like a soldier", they mustn't move. If you have more than one child, make it a race to do the action first. If they get it wrong, they get tickled. Try, "Simon says:"

- "Play a black note on the piano."
- "Clap three times."
- "Sing a high note."
- "Play two notes on the xylophone."
- "Copy this rhythm…"

Then let them have a go at giving *you* instructions and get ready to do some pretty silly things.

Playing any instrument will involve a complex combination of actions, so, if they're older or particularly expert at this game, you could even start demanding more than one action (along the lines of rubbing your tummy while patting your head):

- "Blow the whistle while turning in a circle."
- "Bang the drum with your left hand and shake the maraca in your right hand."

You can give any type of instruction, even non-musical (jump, sit down, wiggle your bottom), and it will still be developing their physical control and coordination, which are important skills for playing music later.

On three…

This is a variation on 'Simon Says'. You say, "On three, put your hand on your head", then count to three and they have to do it as quickly as possible. (I love how simply counting to three makes any instruction instantly more fun to follow.) Try the following:

- Clap your hands
- Lie on the floor
- Sing 'Old MacDonald Had a Farm'
- Sit on the piano stool
- Play one note with each hand
- Rattle the tambourine
- Put your shoes and coat on (sneaky)

Again, if you have more than one player, the slowest gets tickled all over, or a raspberry on their tummy.

Turn up your heartbeat

Pick your favourite high-energy track, turn the volume up and have a short dance competition. The silliest, most hilarious dancing wins. Then sit down together and feel your heartbeats.

- Talk about whether their heart is beating fast or slow.
- Discuss why that might be.
- Ask / show where you can each feel your pulse in your bodies.

There are no right answers here – the aim is just to get them noticing and thinking about it.

Optional bonus experiment: see what happens if you do some slow, deep breaths:

- Does the slow breathing affect the heartrate?
- Does it affect the body or feelings in any other way?

You could call this 'asleep' breathing and get them to think about how someone breathes when sleeping – how do they think it is different to breathing when someone is awake?

This is a fantastic introduction to healthy awareness of the body, without learning specific techniques or explicitly practising 'mindfulness'. For more on breath and body, see Chapter 12.

Slow motion

(with thanks to Tamara Russell and her book *Mindfulness in Motion*)[4]

While you're changing over from one activity or play location to another, see if they can move in slow motion, as if stuck in honey or thick mud, or wading through water. This introduces awareness of movements, which will be crucial if they do go on to play an instrument (or play sport, or act).

It also develops 'inhibitory control skills' (a complex name for the ability to control impulsive or incorrect responses and choose a more appropriate behaviour instead). Building this control is key preparation for any educational or social setting and will also help them to learn independently, which is incredibly valuable.[5]

Here are some actions to experiment with – how slowly can they do each one?

- standing up
- sitting down
- opening and closing a door
- taking a book or toy from the shelf
- climbing a step
- pressing a piano key
- playing the xylophone or shaker

---

[4] Russell, T, *Mindfulness in Motion*, Watkins 2015.

[5] Please see '*Resources*'.

Super-slow walking

A walking-focused variation on Slow Motion.

- Design a path around the room.

- Walk along your path as slowly as physically possible – lifting the foot, moving it forward, placing it down, lifting the other foot…

- Try slow-motion running outside. If you're lucky, this one might buy you a few minutes of peace while they try to figure out the logistics of slow running.

- As a variation, shout: "Freeze!" at any point. They have to freeze wherever they are, ideally with one foot in the air. This would be like a slow-motion, walking version of Musical Statues (see page 88).

(This one is adapted from Susan Kaiser Greenland's movement-meditation exercise 'Slow and Silent Walking' in her book *The Mindful Child,* which I highly recommend.[6])

---

[6] Kaiser Greenland, S, *The Mindful Child*, Atria 2013.

Morning play-along

If you find yourself getting fed up with singing the same nursery rhyme "again… again… again…" you could spend a bit of time sitting together and slowly working out the tune on the piano, xylophone, keyboard app, or any other instrument. It doesn't matter if you don't know how to play the tune – just treat it as an experiment to work on together. Pick a starting note and then ask whether the next note is higher or lower. If they don't know, try a few options and see what sounds the most plausible to you. It really doesn't matter how accurate the result is; the aim is simply to teach them to have a go and listen to the shapes of the melody. They will treasure a bit of time working with you on a joint project. Once they've had enough, let it go – they may well come back to it of their own accord later.

Here are a few simple tunes to try:

- ♫ Old Macdonald Had a Farm
- ♫ Incy Wincy Spider
- ♫ I'm a Little Teapot
- ♫ Hickory Dickory Dock
- ♫ Humpty Dumpty
- ♫ Wind the Bobbin Up
- ♫ Bingo (There Was a Man Who Had a Dog)

Musical charades

It's wonderful for children to start feeling music and emotion in their body, and to become comfortable with moving and coordinating their limbs. By acting out what they hear, through expressive movement and dance, your little ones will also start to hone their awareness of the character and style of music. They may come to this very naturally with little prompting, or you might need to demonstrate some options and talk a bit about what they can hear and what they think it sounds like. Is it energetic or slow, angry or relaxing, happy or sad? What do they think might be happening? Try:

- Sweeping an arm one way then the other for smooth music
- Jumping up and down for loud music
- Pointy, stabby elbows for short notes
- Scurrying mouse feet for fast music
- Fairy tiptoes with floating arms for quiet music
- Little shakes of the hands in all directions for exciting music

This game would work well with the radio on, *alongside* other toys or activities. That way you get a variety of music and can dance intermittently without the pressure of continuing for a whole piece. Alternatively, a playlist of programmatic music (music with a story or narrative) is great, as you have titles, images or events to base your expressive movement on. For example:

> ♪ **Schumann: Kinderszenen (13 Scenes from Childhood)** ⏵23 for piano - within these, try *Blind Man's Buff, Dreaming*, or *Knight of the Hobbyhorse* (my recommended recording: Alfred Brendel)

8: Morning rhythm and wriggles

♪ **Mussorgsky: Pictures at an Exhibition** ●24 – many musical 'pictures', including *The Gnome* and *Ballet of Unhatched Chicks*, for either piano (Evgeny Kissin) or orchestra (Sir Simon Rattle & Berlin Philharmonic Orchestra)

♪ **John Adams: Short Ride in a Fast Machine** ●25 for orchestra (Marin Alsop & Bournemouth Symphony Orchestra)

♪ **Vaughan Williams: The Lark Ascending** ●26 for violin with orchestra (Tamsin Waley-Cohen)

♪ **Chopin: 'Winter Wind' Etude** ●27 for piano (Nikolai Lugansky)

The Happy Music Play Book

Our family's favourite activities: morning rhythm

Date	Name of game	Reaction
……………	…………………………	…………………………………
……………	…………………………	…………………………………
……………	…………………………	…………………………………
……………	…………………………	…………………………………
……………	…………………………	…………………………………
……………	…………………………	…………………………………
……………	…………………………	…………………………………
……………	…………………………	…………………………………
……………	…………………………	…………………………………
……………	…………………………	…………………………………
……………	…………………………	…………………………………
……………	…………………………	…………………………………
……………	…………………………	…………………………………
……………	…………………………	…………………………………

9 Top ten under-a-minute

Sometimes all it takes is a moment of connection or creativity as you go about your day. Here are my favourite mini-ideas for incorporating a bit of music, sound or rhythm at any time, for toddlers and up.

1. Match the pitch

When you hear everyday objects and sounds, see if you can match the pitch with your voice. This is a fun way to demonstrate the idea of 'singing in tune', i.e. blending your own voice with an external sound. Don't worry too much about whether you get the pitch right – you'll probably get more accurate with practice. After a while, your child will start joining in and you can try to find the right pitch together. Again, don't stress about how 'correct' their result is; it's the overall concept and chance to experiment that's useful.

Some sounds to try imitating:

- Washing machine
- Hand dryer
- A rubbish truck beeping
- Doorbell
- Hoover
- Coffee grinder
- Lawnmower
- Electric drill
- Microwave

2. Dance together

If some music is playing, you can help them to dance in time by holding hands; mainly, though, just have fun and wiggle everything. They will really love seeing you dance and laugh, and trying to copy your dance moves.

3. Silly song questions

If you need to ask a boring question or give an instruction, try singing it in the silliest way you can think of. For example, "HAVE YOU GOT YOUR PANTS ON?????" as a highly dramatic opera singer, complete with wobbling voice. Or whisper "Oh, where are your *shoes*, dun dun dun, Oh, where are your *shoes*?" to the James Bond theme tune ("…dun dun dun, FOUND THEM!"). The sillier the better. This is wonderful for diffusing tension if you are feeling stressed or frustrated and they're simply not listening to you. Remember the research on how they pay more attention to singing than normal speaking.

You could even encourage them to sing their response and improvise a full getting-dressed operatic tableau. You'll end up laughing *and* ready to leave.

4. Sirens

Show them how to make a huge siren with their voice: swoop right from the bottom of your voice to the top and back again – a giant fire engine! This will allow them to discover the full range of their voice and gain confidence producing sound. Once they've got the hang of it (you may regret showing them this after the fiftieth time) you could try to replicate the sound on the piano using a glissando (sliding up or down all the keys with the back of your hand).

5. Drumming

Find as many drumming surfaces around the house as you can and drum some very simple rhythms together. I wouldn't give them any instructions – just start tapping and see what they do. If they drum a rhythm you can try to copy them. Or you can initiate a rhythm and see if they join in. Try this on either side of a closed door and you will get no end of giggling.

Possible drumming surfaces:

- as mentioned, a door
- the floor
- sofa cushions
- the stairs
- someone's knees
- water in the bath ("GENTLY, LAURENCE!")

6. Body drums

A more intellectually engaged variation on Drumming, for slightly older kiddos. Use their body as your set of bongos. I often do this when I'm waking mine up from a nap and want to get them out of bed in an affectionate but energetic way, or just while cuddling on the sofa.

- Use different rhythms in different locations, e.g. bass-drum beat on the tummy, faster rhythms on the legs, cymbal crashes using their hands.

- Talk about how different places make different types of drum sounds; for example, their tummy sounds lower and more resonant than their legs. Why do they think that is? Try it on the teddies and see what noises they make: this variety in sound is a fun way to introduce the concept of 'timbre', or the quality of sounds.

7. Ticking clock

Listen together to how a clock ticks regularly, always at the same speed. This is what we call 'pulse' in music. Try to be a clock, too. Think of other examples of regular pulse, or go on a hunt around the house to look for other objects that could make one (you might have a kitchen timer that ticks, or a wind-up toy, for example).

The Happy Music Play Book

8. Tuneful echoes

Just like Babbling Echoes in the Babies section, see if you can sing each other a very simple tune to copy – just two or three notes. The first three notes of 'Three Blind Mice' are a good example, or the first three notes of 'Twinkle Twinkle Little Star'. (Or try either of these backwards.) As you both get more confident, you'll be able to make up some little tunes of your own.

9. Funny lyrics

At some point, children will become highly amused by the concept of rhyming words. For us, the catalyst was the gift of a book called *Oi Frog! (Sit on a log!)* by Kes Gray and Jim Field, but there are many fantastically rhythmic poems and nonsense rhymes to read aloud which they will love. (*On the Ning Nang Nong* by Spike Milligan and *The Owl and the Pussycat* by Edward Lear are two wonderful examples.) You can encourage this creative interest in word play by making up funny lyrics to songs. Make sure that, even if their efforts make NO SENSE, you still enjoy them for what they are - then they'll continue to experiment more and more creatively.

My older son loves making up new words and 'silly versions' of songs he knows. Here is a classic that he made up for baby brother 'Rafey' – the boys were in the bath and we had been singing 'Kookaburra' (proper words on page 85):

> *Kooka-Rafey sitting in the old gum tree,*
> *Merry merry king of the bath is he.*
> *Splash, Kooka-Rafey, splash, Kooka-Rafey,*
> *Gay your bath must be.*

(We also splashed in the relevant places. Cue mad laughter all round.)

This is clearly no great example of poetry, but I was actually surprised and oddly impressed by his spur-of-the-moment thinking. It's amazing what young kids can come up with, given the opportunity.

10. Round and round

Children who are older or more confident with singing might start to enjoy rounds (songs where two or more voices/groups follow each other around, singing the same tune but starting one after the other; if it's a good round, the voices will sound lovely together). I think children find real magic in learning a simple tune and then hearing it transformed into something that sounds beautiful and complex.

Singing rounds is a wonderful introduction to the joy of making music together. It's also quite a challenge of concentration and mental coordination for them to follow their own part and not get distracted and start copying you – fantastic aural and memory training. It would be best at first to have them sing in a team with one adult while another adult follows on. We've got into the habit of doing this with the grandparents as a bedtime song, when we go to stay.

Here are some fun rounds to try. When the first person/team gets to the end of the first line, the next person starts at the beginning, and so on. Continue ad nauseam (or until someone goes wrong and you're all laughing too much to keep singing).

Frère Jacques ○28

Frère Jacques, Frère Jacques,
Dormez-vous? Dormez-vous?
Sonnez les matines, sonnez les matines,
Ding, dang, dong, ding, dang, dong.

London's Burning ○29

London's burning, London's burning,
Fetch the engines, fetch the engines.
Fire fire, fire fire!
Pour on water, pour on water.

Three Blind Mice ○30

Three blind mice, three blind mice,
See how they run, see how they run,
They all ran after the farmer's wife,
Who cut off their tails with a carving knife,
Did you ever see such a thing in your life,
As three blind mice?

Row, Row, Row Your Boat ○31

Row, row, row your boat
Gently down the stream,
Merrily, merrily, merrily, merrily,
Life is but a dream.

(Row, row, row your boat
Gently down the stream,
If you see a crocodile
Don't forget to scream!

Row, row, row your boat
Gently down the river,
If you see a polar bear
Don't forget to shiver!

Row, row, row your boat
Gently to the shore,
If you see a lion
Don't forget to roar!)

Kookaburra ⊙32

Kookaburra sitting in the old gum tree,
Merry merry king of the bush is he.
Laugh, Kookaburra, laugh, Kookaburra,
Gay your life must be!

(Kookaburra sitting in the old gum tree
Eating all the gumdrops he can see
Stop, Kookaburra, Stop, Kookaburra
Leave some there for me!

Kookaburra sitting in the old gum tree,
Counting all the monkeys he can see
Stop, Kookaburra, Stop, Kookaburra,
That's no monkey, that's me!)

The Happy Music Play Book

Our family's favourite activities: under a minute

Date   **Name of game**   **Reaction**

....

....

....

....

....

....

....

....

....

....

....

....

....

10 Rescue kit for grump emergencies

When Laurence was three and Rafe around six months, we had a rainy morning in France, during the late stage of a holiday when all our packed toys had totally lost their interest. I'd exhausted my Duplo creativity building bridges and roads and houses and ramps for a whiney toddler and a baby who only wanted to eat the bricks, and there was still half an hour left until we could reasonably leave the hotel room for a (very) early lunch. Colouring? No. Stickers? No. I spy? NO! In desperation I started singing the silliest, most energetic action songs we knew, getting faster and faster until all the moves got jumbled together. By lunchtime we were all laughing our heads off and I had a well-deserved drink at the restaurant.

I'm not good at spontaneously thinking of ways to distract my children from a tantrum (sometimes the whining makes it hard to think of anything at all). But what I *have* consistently found is that if everyone's feeling a bit under par then music and dancing is the best way to lift us all out of a grump and rescue the day. This chapter is a collection of funny, feel-good diversions to pull out at those sticky moments. If you're sudden and silly enough about it, you'll surprise them so much that they'll forget what they were moaning about.

Musical statues

A classic – but easy to forget if you haven't played it since childhood! You'll need something to play music out loud on.

- When the music starts everyone dances as ridiculously as possible.

- Randomly press pause; when the music stops, all dancers have to immediately freeze where they are, whatever their position.

- Restart the music and start dancing again.

- If you're playing with one child, either dance together or take it in turns controlling the music for each other to dance. You could make up a forfeit (kisses or tickles!) if someone moves or wobbles in the silence.

- In a group, the 'music-master' inspects all players to see who is moving or didn't freeze quickly enough, and those players are out and must sit down. Continue until only the winner is left dancing.

- **Bonus:** You could call out a theme for the dancing, such as animals, or different sports, or fire engines, or having hot potatoes under your feet…

This game is very funny but also develops 'inhibitory control skills'. Please refer to page 71 on this topic.

One step back

A variation on musical statues.

- March in time to the music, then randomly shout out a funny 'signal word' (e.g. "Sausage", "Yelp!", "Pip!" – get them to join in with thinking up the silliest word possible).

- Instead of freezing at the signal, they have to take a step back in their marching before continuing.

- You could also do a version where they change direction on the signal. I suspect they'd particularly love seeing you do this at their signal, if you've got the energy…

This is another one for the old inhibitory control skills (as above). For guidance on marching in time, see page 64.

Turn the music up

This seems to be a recurring theme… but blasting out some jolly music is just the best pick-me-up, and conveniently drowns out the whining. Sorry, can't hear you, too busy dancing. I keep a stack of emergency CDs by the hi-fi rather than wasting time looking for a fun playlist. My emergency CD stack right now is as follows:

- ♪ **Tea Dance – 1920s, 30s, 40s Vintage Tea Party (Artie Shaw & various artists)**
- ♪ **The Great American Big Bands (Glenn Miller & various artists)**
- ♪ **Do You Love Me (Now That I Can Dance) (The Contours)** - this album includes that song from Dirty Dancing…
- ♪ **Quintet of the Hot Club of France (Stephane Grappelli & Django Reinhardt)**
- ♪ **Dixieland Jazz (Sam Levine)**
- ♪ **Hello, I Must Be Going (Phil Collins)**
- ♪ **Café do Brasil (Oscar Pereira Band)**
- ♪ **1962-1966 (The Beatles)**
- ♪ **Buena Vista Social Club (Buena Vista Social Club)**

It's not the most varied emergency collection, but it works for us! The boys both took their first dancing steps to Dixieland Jazz.

It might be fun to order some glowsticks to keep hidden somewhere. Then if you have a seriously bad day you can turn the lights out, close the curtains and have a disco. Or if you need a laugh, search for 'Dancing glow sticks kids fun' on Youtube and recreate with your own sulkers.

10: Rescue kit for grump emergencies

Dance your body parts

We did this for our own amusement when Laurie was starting to learn the parts of his body; if some music came on, we'd try to get him to dance with his head or his arms or legs. It was quite sweet and funny (also useful for waiting around in airports). But it would work just as well for older ones.

- While you're having your dance party, shout out different bits of the body and see if they can dance them in isolation. Bottom? Elbows? Eyebrows? Ears? That should give you a good twenty minutes of entertainment. Meanwhile, you'll be contributing to their physical freedom, strength and coordination, as well as expressiveness and creativity through their body.

- You could do a more systematic variation if you think this would appeal to your child, a bit like the famous 'body scan' for physical awareness. Start with the toes, then the feet and ankles, then the legs, knees, hips, etc., getting them to wiggle each bit in turn.

Silliest action songs

All of these songs have fun dances or actions, which as well as distracting a child from their bad mood will work up lots of nice endorphins. You'll also be building their sense of rhythm, coordination, concentration and memory.

Pirate Ship ⊙33

When I was one, I sucked my thumb, (suck your thumb)
The day I went to sea.
I climbed aboard a pirate ship (climb a rope ladder)
And the Captain said to me:
'We're going this way, that way, (lean right, left…)
Forwards backwards, (…forwards, backwards)
Over the Irish Sea. (make a circle with your torso)

A bottle of rum to fill my tum (mime draining a bottle)
And that's the life for me'. (shade your eyes and look out to sea)

When I was two, I buckled my shoe…

When I was three, I scraped my knee…

When I was four, I swam ashore…

When I was five, I learned to dive…

When I was six, I gathered sticks…

When I was seven, I went to Devon…

When I was eight, I was almost late…

When I was nine, I was feeling fine…

When I was ten, I started again…

Head, Shoulders, Knees and Toes ◐34

Place the hands on each body part in turn.

Head, shoulders, knees and toes, knees and toes,
Head, shoulders, knees and toes, knees and toes,
And eyes and ears and mouth and nose,
Head, shoulders, knees and toes, knees and toes.

Ring a Ring o' Roses ◐35

Join hands and circle around until the final line, when everyone falls on the floor.

Ring a ring o' roses
A pocketful of posies
a-tishoo, a-tishoo
We all fall down.

Grand Old Duke of York ◐36

March in time, then scramble somewhere high, somewhere low and somewhere midway for 'up', 'down' and 'halfway up'.

Words on page 51.

This is the Way the Lady Rides ▶37

(same tune as 'Here we go round the Mulberry Bush', page 48)

(Gently, bouncing the child on your knee in time)

This is the way the lady rides,
Trippety tee, trippety tee,
This is the way the lady rides,
Trippety, trippety tee.

(Faster, bouncing more energetically)

This is the way the gentleman rides,
Gallopy gallop, gallopy gallop,
This is the way the gentleman rides,
Gallopy, gallopy gallop.

(As fast as you can, wobbling them side to side)

This is the way the farmer rides,
Hobbledy Hoi, Hobbledy Hoi,
This is the way the farmer rides,
And down into the ditch!!!

(Make them 'fall off' the horse to shrieks of laughter.)

You could add some of your own characters with different styles and speeds of riding. We like the businessman rushing with his briefcase.

Did You Ever See a Lassie ⊙38

Hold hands and form a rotating circle. On the lines 'Go this way and that way', one player chooses an action which the others imitate. Change the direction of the circle, and the action-chooser, for the next verse.

Did you ever see a lassie
A lassie, a lassie
Did you ever see a lassie
Go this way and that?
Go this way and that way
Go this way and that way
Did you ever see a lassie
Go this way and that?

Did you ever see a laddie
A laddie, a laddie
Did you ever see a laddie
Go this way and that?
Go this way and that way
Go this way and that way
Did you ever see a laddie
Go this way and that?

Hop Little Bunnies ●39

The bunnies lie down and pretend to sleep, then wake up, jump up, and hop around as energetically as possible. You can change 'hop' to 'jump' or 'skip' (or any other action) for following verses.

See the bunnies sleeping til it's nearly noon,
Shall we wake them with a merry tune?
They're so still, are they ill?
No! Wake up bunnies!
Hop little bunnies, hop, hop, hop
Hop little bunnies, hop, hop, hop
Hop little bunnies, hop, hop, hop
Hop little bunnies, hop and stop!

Dingle Dangle Scarecrow ●40

When all the cows were sleeping,	(lie down sleeping)
And the sun had gone to bed,	
Up jumped the scarecrow	(jump up)
And this is what he said	(hands on hips)
I'm a dingle, dangle scarecrow	(wave arms side to side)
With a flippy, floppy hat,	(nod head side to side)
I can shake my hands like this,	(shake arms)
I can shake my feet like that.	(shake or kick legs)

10: Rescue kit for grump emergencies

One Finger, One Thumb ⊙41

Hold out the relevant body part (or do the action) in time with the tune – you'll either work up a good sweat or get into a complete muddle.

One finger, one thumb, keep moving
One finger, one thumb, keep moving
One finger, one thumb, keep moving
We'll all be merry and bright.

One finger, one thumb, one arm, keep moving…

One finger, one thumb, one arm, one leg, keep moving…

One finger, one thumb, one arm, one leg, one nod of the head, keep moving…

One finger, one thumb, one arm, one leg, one nod of the head, sit down, stand up, keep moving…

One finger, one thumb, one arm, one leg, one nod of the head, sit down, stand up and turn around, keep moving…

⭐

Calm them with breathing

If your child is very upset (rather than just in a generally bad mood), a good thing to try is breathing in for four and then out for four. You could say, "It's OK, take some big breaths, it will make you feel better. Shall we breathe together? Breathe in… (count to four in your head or out loud) … and breathe out (count to four) … breathe in… and breathe out." Continue until they are calmer. They might not join in at first but will gradually pick it up. You could combine the breathing with then singing one of the lullabies from Chapter 16 for an even more comforting effect.

As well as an understanding of breathing, which is a beautiful thing to give to a child in order to set them up with emotional awareness and resilience in life, this is a very first introduction to regular musical meter (counting to four over and over).

Bear in mind that this might not work the first time if they're already in a bad mood, but once you've got the hang of it together it will definitely be useful in grumpy situations! For more tips on breathing to calm and comfort, see Chapter 12.

10: Rescue kit for grump emergencies

The Silly Sausage Orchestra

Gather any instruments you have in the house (including makeshift ones such as pasta or lentils in a Tupperware, saucepans with wooden spoons, and DIY recycling instruments – see page 30) and play them in the silliest ways you can come up with. Here are some initial ideas:

- Lying on your back
- Play a shaker with your feet
- Toot the recorder while wiggling your bottom
- Play with your head touching the floor
- Hold the instrument upside down
- Play the piano while facing the other way
- Play while also singing loudly

- Think of an animal and imagine how they would play the instrument (e.g. floppy and slippery like a fish, loudly trumpeting like an elephant, hiding under the table like a mouse, jumping up and down like a monkey)

- Imitate a character from one of their books or films

This is a really great way to encourage light-hearted, unselfconscious music-making. Because they're relaxed and smiling, your children will be using their body in the most natural way, with no tension (a wonderful basis for playing any instrument). Thinking of funny things to do also develops creativity and physical coordination.

⭐

Sing it wrong

Pick a song and sing it in an odd way – in my experience, guaranteed to make them laugh, even if just in surprise.

- Use a stupid voice
- Sing either very slowly or super-fast
- Sing it in a very low or very high pitch (hilarious)
- Get it wrong very obviously, either ending on the wrong note or swapping the words for something incongruous, e.g.: 'The grand old duke of Birmingham with his ten thousand cows.'
- Very short (staccato) notes, as if you're laughing
- Upside down: swap high notes for low and low notes for high (this is a pretty good brain teaser for you and you can see if they're able to work out what's happened to the tune. Don't panic; it's still interesting even if not a very accurate inversion!).

This also works well if you hear them singing something they know, or making up a little tune: you can echo them using one of these funny methods. In due course, they will probably start trying out the same effects, to see if they can make *you* laugh.

Sofa sailing

If all else fails, make a boat with your sofa, a duvet, a yoga mat, some cushions or a laundry basket and have a sea-faring singalong. Maybe make some sailor hats for good measure. This is great if you have more than one grumpy child on your hands. Here is a possible sea-themed sequence:

Pirate Ship ○42

Turn back to page 92 for the words

Row, Row, Row Your Boat ○43

Turn back to page 84 for the words

Drunken Sailor ○44

What shall we do with the drunken sailor?
What shall we do with the drunken sailor?
What shall we do with the drunken sailor?
Early in the morning?

Hooray, and up she rises
Hooray, and up she rises
Hooray, and up she rises
Early in the morning

Dance to Your Daddy ○45

Dance to your Daddy, my little laddie,
Dance to your Daddy, my little man.
You shall have a fishy on a little dishy,
You shall have a fishy when the boat comes in.

10: Rescue kit for grump emergencies

My Bonnie Lies Over the Ocean ○46

*My Bonnie lies over the ocean,
My Bonnie lies over the sea,
My Bonnie lies over the ocean,
Oh, bring back my Bonnie to me.*

*Bring back, bring back,
Oh, bring back my Bonnie to me, to me,
Bring back, bring back,
Oh, bring back my Bonnie to me.*

A Sailor Went to Sea ○47

*A sailor went to sea, sea, sea
To see what he could see, see, see
But all that he could see, see, see
Was the bottom of the deep blue sea, sea, sea!*

You can think of things that the sailor might see in the sea, for example:

*But all that he could see, see, see
Was a shark in the deep blue sea, sea, sea!*

Hopefully by then it'll be time for lunch.

The Happy Music Play Book

Our family's favourite activities: emergencies

Date	Name of game	Reaction
....	....	....
....	....	....
....	....	....
....	....	....
....	....	....
....	....	....
....	....	....
....	....	....
....	....	....
....	....	....
....	....	....
....	....	....
....	....	....

11 Rescue kit for exhausted parents
Quiet activities for when you need a sit down and a cup of tea

"I don't know about other parents, but I'm often exhausted so anything I can do to engage him from an armchair usually works very well for me," a tired friend with an energetic little boy told me. I'm sure she's not alone!

This chapter is for anyone who just needs a little breather. Hopefully some of these ideas will help you get a few peaceful minutes once or twice a month, in which to drink your coffee without spilling it, rest your hard-working knees / back / arms / head (delete as appropriate) and still feel virtuous about doing something vaguely educational.

Big and small

The idea here is that your child bounces around expressing what they hear through movement, while you sit comfortably and encourage / commentate. You'll need something to play music out loud on.

They get as large as possible when the music is loud: stretching up to the ceiling, waving their arms around, or maybe jumping as high as they can.

Become as small and still as possible when it's quiet: crouching down on the floor, rolling into a ball, lying down or even hiding completely.

They can choose what to become in between these two extremes.

There's no right or wrong here; however they hear or express the music is valid, even if it doesn't match your view of what is loud or quiet. But it might help them to loosen up if some teddies are on hand to join in and possibly demonstrate the difference between loud and quiet if necessary. If the game disintegrates into rolling on the floor, that's good too.

The best music for this is something with lots of contrast, like one of these:

- ♪ **Dukas: The Sorceror's Apprentice** for orchestra (my recommended recording: Sir Alexander Gibson & Royal Scottish National Orchestra) ◐48

- ♪ **Berlioz: 'Marche au Supplice' from *Symphonie Fantastique*** for orchestra (Sir Colin Davis & London Symphony Orchestra) ◐49

- ♪ **Brahms: Hungarian Dance no. 2** for orchestra (Claudio Abbado & Vienna Philharmonic Orchestra) ◐50

11: Rescue kit for exhausted parents

♪ **Brahms: Hungarian Dance no. 6** for orchestra
(Claudio Abbado & Vienna Philharmonic Orchestra)
◐51

♪ **Ravel: 'Scarbo' from** *Gaspard de la Nuit* for piano
(Martha Argerich) – this is about a goblin who keeps appearing and disappearing at night, so a good one for expressing sound through movement. ◐52

♪ **John Williams: 'Hedwig's Theme' from** *Harry Potter* (Gustavo Dudamel & Los Angeles Philharmonic)
◐53

♪ **Mussorgsky: 'Cattle' from** *Pictures at an Exhibition* for orchestra (Valery Gergiev & Mariinsky Orchestra)
◐54

It might be an idea to make a playlist for this and any other favourite games, so that you don't have to search for something each time you play the game. I've never been organised enough yet though.

Props department

Send them off to find props for songs they know. The best timewaster I can think of is 'This Old Man' as it has ten verses with very random props needed. I would sing it verse by verse and each time you get to 'He played knick knack on my…' get them to search the house for an appropriate toy or object. You obviously won't have kneebones, beehives or heaven hanging around your house, but that's even better – they'll have to use their imagination to come up with a stand-in (a bee or an angel, for example). You could also let them loose in the recycling bin to find some items with which to make their own props.

This Old Man ○55

This old man, he plays one,
He plays knick knack on my thumb,
With a knick knack paddy wack
Give a dog a bone,
This old man comes rolling home.

This old man, he plays two,
He plays knick knack on my shoe…

…three… on my knee…

…four… on my door…

…five… on my hive…

…six… on my sticks…

…seven… up in heaven…

…eight… on the gate…

…nine… on my vine…

…ten…all over again…

If it takes them two or three minutes each time, that's almost half an hour of armchair relaxation. (You could also do this as a treasure hunt by hiding specific props around the house or garden, but that requires quite a lot more input from you!)

Other songs to try:

Pirate Ship ○56 (words on page 92)

Wheels on the Bus ○57 (make up new verses involving objects such as 'The children on the bus they read their books' or 'The chefs on the bus they wash their pans')

London Bridge is Falling Down ○58

London Bridge is falling down,
Falling down, falling down,
London Bridge is falling down,
My fair lady.

Build it up with wood and clay,
Wood and clay, wood and clay,
Build it up with wood and clay,
My fair lady.

Wood and clay will wash away…

Build it up with iron and steel…

Iron and steel will bend and bow…

Build it up with silver and gold…

Silver and gold will be stolen away…

Send a man to watch all night…

Most of the simpler nursery rhymes like 'Mary Had a Little Lamb', 'Incy Wincy Spider', 'Hot Cross Buns' etc. will also work well.

The Happy Music Play Book

Mini-pendulums

If they haven't seen a grandfather clock before, first show them how a pendulum works by tying something heavy to a string and letting it swing to and fro. This in itself should entertain for a good amount of time - and bonus points for the physics lesson. Once they've seen how it sways side to side with a regular rhythm, see if they can now be a pendulum.

- Have them sit down cross-legged on the floor.
- Make a slow regular clock sound for them — either a ticking sound with your mouth, or perhaps using a gong, a bell, a note on the xylophone or piano, or even a fork on a glass.
- Each time they hear the sound they tilt their torso to the side, alternating right and left.

This is great for the posture, but mainly for developing their sense of pulse. You could have fun speeding up the pendulum, or really slowing it down a lot.

Vary this by having a different sound (e.g. a drum or a saucepan, or a different note on the piano or xylophone).

When they hear this different sound, they have to find the middle of their bottom again, so they're perfectly balanced, and wait there until the normal clock pulse starts again.

11: Rescue kit for exhausted parents

Teddy concert

Set up a little concert hall with any instruments (real or makeshift) that you can gather on one side of the room and some chairs for yourself (you get the VIP armchair, of course) and all the teddies. Arranging this will probably hold their attention for at least five or ten minutes. Depending on how extravagant you're feeling, you could include 'music' on a stand, dressing up clothes for their dinner jacket or gown, or even some stage curtains. Then let them play you a concert for as long as it amuses them. All you have to do is to be very interested in what they've played, ask them about their piece and show you enjoyed it however refined (or otherwise) the concert is. The teddies might also need some help clapping.

When they get fed up with this, one of the animals could have a turn playing the instruments, or perhaps you'll get Pavarotti Penguin, 'The Fluffs' string quartet, or the SOS (Symphony Orchestra of Soft-bears).

If you want to stretch this game out for a few more minutes, make a stage for the teddies out of Duplo or Lego. Remember the steps at the side for them to get onto the stage, and how about a Duplo frame for some stage curtains, made from two scarves?

11: Rescue kit for exhausted parents

Musical emojis

This can be used both for helping children tune into and express their mood and emotions on different days and also to help with listening to music and starting to talk about its character or mood.

- Cut a piece of A4 paper or card into squares.

- Draw different facial expressions on each square, as well as some pictures to represent musical character. (Get them to colour in the squares as well for a few extra minutes' peace.)

- For example, fast = a plane, slow = a snail, exciting = fireworks, sleepy = the moon. Include any other moods or emotions you think of.

- Play some music and ask your child to choose which picture the music makes them think of.

- They can also choose which face or picture best represents them each day.

Breathing in bars

Pick a simple song that they know well. Experiment together, seeing if, while one of you sings, the other can breathe in for the first and third lines and breathe out for the second and fourth (etc.). So for example, if you are singing:

Three blind mice (they breathe in)

Three blind mice (they breathe out)

See how they run (in)

See how they run (out)

They all ran after the farmer's wife (in)

Who cut off their tails with a carving knife (out)

11: Rescue kit for exhausted parents

Did you ever see such a thing in your life (in)

As three blind mice? (out)

Each of these lines is equivalent to a bar of music (for non-musicians: bars and barlines are the way we divide up written music into regular measures), so they are effectively breathing in bars even though they don't know what these are yet!

At first it might be helpful to listen to the song and do the breathing together.

Alternatively, take turns to sing and to breathe. It may take a while to make sense, so don't worry about doing it 'right', just go on experimenting as long as it's engaging.

This is a great test of coordination and concentration.

It will give them a fantastic foundation on which to build when they start reading music. Understanding the concept of a bar as a regular division of music, and getting used to playing a musical phrase as a physical breath are both core skills for musical playing.

Mantra notes

Another breathing one with a nice calming effect.

- Get them to choose a note on the piano (or keyboard, app, xylophone, triangle etc.). It can be any note. This is their musical 'mantra', or repeating sound.

- Take a breath in together, then on the exhale they play and hold their chosen note.

- Inhale, and then on the exhale they play the note again. Keep going until it feels easy and relaxing.

There are all sorts of variations on this to try over time if they enjoy it and are gaining confidence.

- Choose two notes and play one on each inhale and one on each exhale, so the notes are constantly alternating.

- They could play one in each hand, e.g. C with the left hand and G with the right hand. Or choose neighbouring notes to play with the same hand, e.g. C and D alternating with the right hand. Now they are playing a (slow) trill.

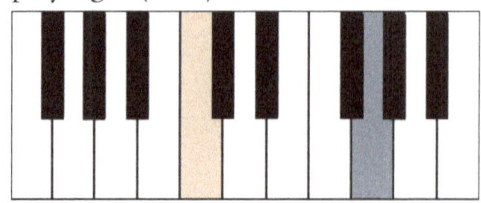

- Play a new note on each exhale.

- Choose two (or three) notes at once, instead of just one, and play them together on each exhale. They are now playing a chord!

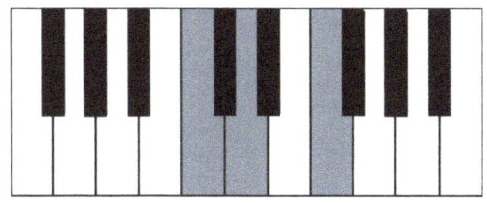

- For older children, or those comfortable with the previous variation, choose two chords. Play one on the inhales and one on the exhales, so that the chords are alternating. This would work best with one chord for each hand, for example C and E for the right hand, alternating with G and B for the left hand.

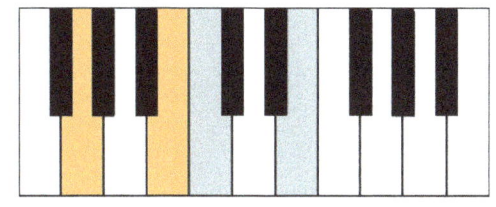

Neither of you need to worry about how it sounds – just help them focus on the breathing and the feeling of playing the notes.

This activity is about integrating calm and relaxed breathing into the act of playing an instrument, leading to a relaxed body and natural, easy musicality. It will also provide children with an early experience of 'flow' (relaxed concentration). Refer to Chapters 2 and 4 for more on both these aspects of musical performance skills.

Colour the music

I'd like to thank one of my earliest piano teachers, the composer Wendy Hiscocks, for introducing me to this when I was very young. I still remember the experience vividly.

- Get out some crayons or paint and some paper. A1 size paper would be awesome so you can get on the floor and feel really free.

- Listen to some music and talk with them a little bit about what colour or shape they think the music sounds like.

- Don't worry about the answers, it doesn't really matter what they say. It's just an opportunity for some closer, more engaged listening. You might be surprised by how perceptive some of their observations can be, though.

- Then start 'colouring the music' on the paper, using swishes, swirls, strong strokes, angular zig zags or gentle wavy wiggles. If it sounds grumpy or scary you could use

11: Rescue kit for exhausted parents

darker colours, or bright colours for high or energetic music. They will probably really enjoy seeing you do your own, too, so you could do them side by side. They may also take inspiration from the kinds of shapes you make - the bigger and bolder, the better.

- *The Planets* by Gustav Holst would be good for this as the music is so vibrant and most children will enjoy the space theme.

Musical films to watch together

Here are some lovely, child-friendly musical films for a rainy afternoon - younger children might not last all the way through the films but we often split the viewing between two or more days. They'll enjoy learning some new songs.

- ♪ **Mary Poppins** the original, featuring Julie Andrews.
- ♪ **The Sound of Music** my favourite film of all time, stuffed with fantastic music and featuring Julie Andrews again. (Caution: the Nazis marching in and later trying to stop the family escaping would be too scary for my four-year-old, so I stop the film after Maria and Captain von Trapp get married. Both boys absolutely love watching the children sing, especially the song *Doe, A Deer, A Female Deer*.)
- ♪ **Easter Parade** song and dance with Fred Astaire and Judy Garland
- ♪ **Singin' in the Rain** one of the best musicals, with Gene Kelly.

- ♪ **Oscar's Orchestra** In a Vienna where music has been banned, Oscar the Piano rallies his friends Eric the Triangle, Trevor the Tuba and Monty the Violin, as they set out on many adventures in their quest to bring music back into the world. Featuring the voice of Dudley Moore as Oscar and music by many famous composers, this classic TV series is hard to find but available second hand. (Caution: the evil dictator Thadius Vent may be a little scary for younger children.)

- ♪ **Tom and Jerry: The Cat Concerto** (Tom tries to play a piano concerto while Jerry sleeps inside the piano. Chaos ensues.)

- ♪ **Tom and Jerry: The Cat Above and the Mouse Below** (Tom is an opera singer, disturbing Jerry's sleep below the stage. Similar result.)

- ♪ **Fantasia** Walt Disney's timeless masterpiece brings some of the most famous classical music to life with imaginative storylines and mesmerising visual sequences. (Caution: be on hand in case you need to skip parts for more sensitive children - I do remember finding the multiplying brooms in '*The Sorceror's Apprentice*' rather frightening!)

11: Rescue kit for exhausted parents

Our family's favourite activities: exhausted parents

Date	Name of game	Reaction
....	....	....
....	....	....
....	....	....
....	....	....
....	....	....
....	....	....
....	....	....
....	....	....
....	....	....
....	....	....
....	....	....
....	....	....
....	....	....

12 Breathing and movement for mini-musicians
Explore, calm and comfort

This short chapter focuses on the mind and body, through breathing experiments and fun, easy yoga. You may wonder why I've included this in a book about music; the answer is that awareness of what's happening in the body is absolutely central to music-making, as well as to emotional and physical health in general. These activities and shapes will help your child develop a strong mind-body connection and learn how to use their limbs and their breath creatively: valuable in music, and in all artistic and sporting endeavours.

BREATHING

Awareness of the breath, and the ability to use it in challenging situations, is such a useful life skill. It will also provide a great basis for understanding the natural ebb and flow of music, as musical phrases often correspond with the natural breath. Proper breathing is equally important for relaxed and healthy singing, or for playing an instrument.

Learning to breathe properly

In an ideal world, we want to get our children breathing deeply, calmly and smoothly into the tummy and ribs, so that they fill with air (like a balloon) on the inhale. You can show them how to do this by lying down, side by side, and putting your hands on your tummies. When you breathe in you can both watch your hands moving upwards and slightly apart. You could even sit a small stuffed animal on your tummies, to show how the stomach rises during a full inhale (teddy goes up), and sinks back down on a full exhale (teddy goes down). They might like to imagine rocking the teddy to sleep with their breaths.

You can help your child to explore the different feelings of breathing deeply into the tummy, the ribs (this one feels like the ribs and the sides of the torso are expanding) and the chest (this is what children generally use if they consciously 'take a big breath in', with the shoulders going up and the tummy sucking in). See if you can do each one separately. And then see if you can breathe into all three together.

12: Breathing and movement for mini-musicians

Counting breaths

Try different methods of counting your breaths.

- First, experiment with simply breathing in and out on alternate counts (count slowly: in on 1, out on 2, etc.)

- Then, try counting down from 10 instead of up from 1.

- Now try in for two counts, out for two.

- In for three, out for three.

- In for four, out for four.

This is their foundation for understanding bars of two, three or four beats if they later start reading music.

- See how many counts you can keep the breath going without bursting!

- You could ask them to breathe in for four and out for six – this is a well-known technique for calming down.

Talk about which methods you each prefer. I learned this in preparation for labour and giving birth; I found it interesting that everyone in the class had a very different experience of each method and of which ones they found relaxing.

Calm them with breathing

This is in 'Chapter 10 Rescue Kit for Grump Emergencies' but I'm going to pop it in here as well, to sit with the other Breathing activities.

If your child is very upset (rather than just in a generally bad mood), a good thing to try is breathing in for four and then out for four. You could say, "It's OK, take some big breaths, it will make you feel better. Shall we breathe together? Breathe in… (count to four in your head or out loud) … and breathe out (count to four) … breathe in… and breathe out." Continue until they are calmer. They might not join in at first but will gradually pick it up. You could combine the breathing with then singing one of the lullabies from Chapter 16 for an even more comforting effect.

If you're able to find a quiet moment to introduce this for the first time in a relaxed way, perhaps before bed, then it might be easier to use subsequently to help them calm down at a moment of frustration or distress. As they grow in confidence you can also encourage them to select times for themselves when they would like to try breathing. We've been doing the basic calm breathing with Laurence since he was one, and my heart swelled with pride and love recently when he was crying over something and sobbed, "Daddy, please can you do the breathing with me?"

Crab & Whale

If you feel that learning to breathe deeply is something you want to enjoy more with your children, I can recommend *Crab & Whale*, by Mark Pallis and Christiane Kerr, which was recommended to me in turn by an educational psychologist. It's a beautifully illustrated short story for young children which explores breathing and the joys of being kind (the crab helps a beached whale to keep calm).

Breathing prompts

If your child is going through an especially anxious phase you could also come up with some 'breathing prompts' (another idea I got from Susan Kaiser Greenland's book *The Mindful Child*[7]) to remind them to take a few deep breaths at certain times. The prompt could be an object that becomes associated with breathing (a soft animal, or a smooth stone), or simply a specific moment in the day when you always take some breaths together, e.g. after brushing their teeth or when they come in the front door.

Lengthening exhales more than the duration of the inhales (for example, in for three, out for four) is great for calming down the nervous system in times of anxiety/grumpiness. Conversely, lengthening or strengthening inhales is a great way to boost energy if you're feeling sleepy or sluggish.

---

[7] Kaiser Greenland, S, *The Mindful Child*, Atria 2013.

YOGA

Making these physical shapes and stretches improves concentration, coordination and awareness of the body, all key elements of future music-making (and simple healthy living). Kids also love to imitate and to play make-believe, and helping them to bring these poses to life with a story or extra details will develop their imagination. This is why I've chosen mostly familiar things such as animals, helicopters and trees, in this section. All the suggestions here have been reviewed and approved by Elena Urioste, violinist and trained yoga teacher.[8]

Yoga will work best with ages three upwards, as by then they can really grasp the instructions, can listen to their bodies and communicate with you easily if something doesn't feel right or is too hard. But if you have more than one child, then younger ones will enjoy joining in and trying to copy their siblings. A few pointers:

- Find a safe, open space to move around, ideally on a carpet or mat to avoid slipping or falling on a hard floor.

- As with anything new, some children may want to watch you a few times before they feel comfortable trying themselves. It's a fun thing to do together anyway and you might even enjoy the stretches yourself.

- Try not to over-correct. If the poses don't look 'perfect', that is just fine. As long as there is no risk of injury (for example: putting weight on their head or neck, over-stretching), then generally, it is best to let your children express the pose however they enjoy it.

- Likewise, let them go at their own pace and don't try to move their body into a position. The best way is to use words and to demonstrate the shape yourself for your little one to copy.

- Remind them to keep breathing, because sometimes when they are really concentrating on balance, for example, they may forget.

---

[8] You can learn more about Elena and her work at **www.elenaurioste.com** and **www.intermissionsessions.com**.

- Smaller ones may struggle at first with balance, so perhaps stand them next to a wall or chair when doing a balancing posture (e.g. tree pose or flying pose).

- Have fun!

Cow and cat

- These two poses go together and are great for stretching out the spine and back.

- Start on all fours with a flat, relaxed back.

- First be a cow in the field, munching on grass, with a big belly hanging down. Allow the belly button to drop towards the floor and the chin and bottom to lift a little as the cow looks at the trees and the grass it's about to eat.

- Now transform into a hissing cat, curling your back up towards the sky and pulling your belly button upwards. Let your head hang down. Round that back up as much as you can - perhaps make some cat sounds while you're there.

- Come back to that first, flat-backed position, then switch between cow and cat a few more times.

Swimming arms

This is a nice way to explore the different muscles and movements around the neck and shoulders, before tension starts to develop in this area as children grow up.

- Standing up, reach one arm in front, then circle it up and behind you as if swimming backstroke, bringing it back down to rest by your side.

- Repeat with the other arm. Try to keep the rest of the body still and relaxed.

- Try the swimming stroke forwards and backwards with each arm.

- When they feel comfortable with the movement, can they do one arm forwards and one arm backwards? This really works on coordination and physical control, concentration and awareness of what feels easy or difficult within the body.

Tree

Tall, grounded and strong: tree pose is great for improving balance, strength and concentration.

- Stand up straight and tall, hands by your sides, finding a still point in front to focus on (this can be an object, a wall, or window).

- Shift your weight into your right foot. Imagine it being a tree root, growing down strongly into the ground. Slowly bring up your left heel to rest against your right inner ankle, or on top of the right foot.

- Stretch your arms up above – you are a growing tree! – or reach them far out to the sides like branches. You could talk about how the branches soak up the sunlight (bonus Biology lesson).

- What type of tree are you? Are you in a forest, a meadow or a park? Try shaking your leaf hands or swaying gently side to side in the breeze.

- Return your leg to the ground and your arms to the sides. Now repeat with the other leg.

Helicopter

It's always fun to be a helicopter, and at the same time to relax the upper body.

- Stand with feet slightly wider than hip-width.

- Turn the whole torso from side to side, from the base of the spine to the top of the head, looking over each shoulder. Allow the arms to swing from side to side, making a circle around the body.

- Start to rev up the engines, finding a speed that feels comfy and airborne. Let the arms really relax so that they flop from side to side, hitting whichever part of the body they land on.

- When you've finished your flight, gradually slow down the turns of the torso until the arms stop swinging.

12: Breathing and movement for mini-musicians

Squeezy shoulders

This would be great to use at any moment of stress or meltdown, just to subtly redirect the emotions and energy.

- With arms hanging by your sides, squeeze the shoulders up to your ears, as high as you can.

- Let them drop back down, as heavy as sacks of potatoes.

- Now add the breath – inhale and hold as you lift and squeeze the shoulders; release them with a big audible exhale. Repeat.

Flying Pose (AKA Warrior 3)

Make this an aeroplane, a rocket or a bird, depending on your child's interests. Flying Pose gives a boost of super-energy and improves balance, but also teaches mental focus and will-power: we learn to keep our mind calmly focused when facing a challenge (here, a challenge of balance).

- Begin standing tall and strong, palms together in front of your heart.

- Slowly lift up one leg behind you, trying not to wobble! Focusing on one point in front will help.

- Hinge from the hips, bringing the upper body and lifted leg parallel to the floor: this makes the aeroplane body.

- Stretch the foot out behind you, like you're pressing it towards the wall: extend with energy back through the foot and forward through the top of the head.

- Keep palms together, or reach your wings out to the sides or in front as you soar through the sky.

- Balance for a few breaths if possible, or until you wobble over, and then repeat on the other side.

Mouse Pose (Child's Pose)

This is a very calming and relaxing pose. It looks like a tiny mouse resting still - perhaps find a small cuddly mouse toy to sit beside your child.

- Start kneeling up tall, then send your bottom back to sit on your heels.

- Take a big breath in, then let it all out as you gently bend over your knees to rest your forehead on the floor in front of you. This makes the lovely round shape of a little mouse.

- You can widen the legs a little if that feels comfier.

- Let the arms rest beside you on the floor and take a few relaxing breaths here while the mouse has a nap.

This little mouse is a good starting point for making small quiet shapes, when playing 'Big and Small' on page 106.

13 Musical mealtimes
Kitchen dancing and conversation-starters to fuel imaginations

We use a lot of music during and around mealtimes, mainly because we're all crammed into our small kitchen and it helps to keep everyone entertained. By diffusing any tension around eating or food, listening to and making music helps us to relax and enjoy the meal process (in this I include parents who are seeing their lovingly prepared food spat out or refused).

Listening to music also provides opportunities for fun and interesting discussions, which can turn teatimes into joyful rather than tedious memories and set your table-kickers up for life with healthy, happy eating habits and associations.

'Dancing in the Kitchen' playlist

I often find the half-hour before tea one of the trickiest times of day, with both boys a little tired, hungry and fed up, each wanting 150% attention from me regardless of the fact that I'm also trying to cook their meal. My first go-to is to put on a really happy album of music; this relaxes me enough that we often end up dancing and cooking together rather than whining and battling. I actually remember that when my brother and I were very small, my mother used Strauss waltzes this same way - those pieces give me warm and fuzzy feelings to this day.

▶ 59

- **Johann Strauss: Waltzes, Polkas & Marches (Wiener Philharmoniker & Willi Boskovsky)** - as swirled and twirled to by me aged three.
  If you like this, try William Tell Overture (Rossini) and 'Can-can' from *Orpheus in the Underworld* (Offenbach)

- **The Road West (Mairtin O'Connor)** - uplifting and catchy tunes from one of Ireland's most respected musicians.
  If you like this, try Riverdance: Music from the Show (Bill Whelan)

- **Graceland (Paul Simon)** - what a classic!

- **Shall We Dance? (John Wilson & his Orchestra)**
  If you like this, try That's Entertainment: A Celebration of the MGM Film Musical (The John Wilson Orchestra)

- **Boogie Woogie Piano (Hamp Garnett)**
  If you like this, try Scott Joplin: Piano Rags, Vol. 2 (Benjamin Loeb)

- **Frixx (Frigg)** - Finnish folk music with fiddles and guitar
  If you like this, try The Road North (Alasdair Fraser)

13: Musical mealtimes

- ♪ **Eric Coates: Orchestral Works, Vol. 1 (BBC Philharmonic Orchestra & John Wilson)** - British light music at its best

- ♪ **Swinging The Blues, Dancing The Ska (Jools Holland and his Rhythm & Blues Orchestra)** - one of my favourites for swinging my boys round the room

- ♪ **Leonard Bernstein: West Side Story Symphonic Dances (Leonard Bernstein & Los Angeles Philharmonic Orchestra)**
  If you like this, try Aaron Copland: 'Hoe-Down' (from Rodeo)

- ♪ **Arturo Márquez: 'Danzón no 2' (Gustavo Dudamel & Simón Bolívar Symphony Orchestra;** there is also a great version by the Teresa Carreno Youth Orchestra of Venezuela, which is fun and inspiring for children to watch)
  If you like this, try Dmitri Shostakovich: 'Festive Overture'

DIY instruments

If you need to get them out from under your feet while you cook, choose a musical instrument from the list below and commission them to make you one out of recycled bottles, boxes, cardboard tubes or other household objects. We have had a French horn made of a plastic water bottle, a cello made from the inside of a cling film roll (a fairly free interpretation, that one), and a watering-can tuba (getting closer). Cymbals can be made from those sticky Velcro hand bats – these lost their shine for me after about the third day of loud 'cymballing'. It really doesn't matter how authentic it looks – the imagination is so powerful at this age. If you're not familiar with an instrument, even better – you can discover it together! They will love it.

13: Musical mealtimes

Instruments to create:

Strings	Woodwind	Brass	Percussion
Violin	Flute	Trumpet	Drumkit
Viola	Clarinet	Trombone	Timpani
Cello	Oboe	Tuba	Marimba
Double bass	Bassoon	French horn	Xylophone
Guitar	Recorder	Euphonium	Glockenspiel
Harp	Saxophone	Tenor horn	Piano
Balalaika	Piccolo	Cornet	Tabla

Keep your DIY instruments so that the teddies can make an orchestra for 'Teddy Concert' (see page 111).

Bonus activities for DIY instruments:

- Find a picture of the instrument your child wants to make and also of someone playing it. It's fun for them to connect the sound they'll hear with an image.

- Then look for some music featuring that instrument – you can find a Spotify playlist by simply searching for the instrument. There's a great jazzy 'tuba' collection, for example, which we enjoy a lot.

- Talk about the character of the instrument: is it low or high? Help them think about why it's the shape and size it is, in order to make that sound. Can you think of any other objects that sound similar, e.g. a foghorn? A bee buzzing? Someone singing? An elephant?

- Older children could draw their version of the instrument, or of themselves playing it.

Tray drumming

At first I thought it was incredibly sweet when Laurie banged on his highchair tray during meals. Then after a few months it started to really annoy me, until I decided to use the opportunity and began copying his rhythms. He was so delighted that it was worth the noise. I did worry occasionally that I was teaching him bad table manners, but he grew out of the banging pretty soon.

So, if you've got a baby or toddler, try playing call and echo on the table or their tray while they eat. You can copy them first, then see if they will pick up on it if you change the rhythm. (See page 43 for a recap on how to make up rhythms.) But I probably wouldn't do it in front of the grandparents.

What am I tapping?

As a variation on the above for older children, tap the rhythm of a favourite song and see if they can guess what song it is. To introduce different types of sound you could tap on the table:

- gently with your hand flat
- with your fingertips, while your wrist rests on the table (as if you're waiting impatiently)
- with two fingernails
- with a pen

Two ways of taking this up a level are:

- tapping only the first line of the song
- making them close their eyes and guess what you're using to tap (this might cause a bit of a delay to the eating… but it's all in the name of fun and music).

LISTENING ACTIVITIES FOR MEALTIME DISCUSSION

How valuable it is for children to learn at an early age to make interesting conversation at the dinner table. The following four activities will provide countless topics for discussion, in which even children as young as two or three can participate. As well as learning more about music and instruments, your child will be able to exchange opinions with you (an empowering experience for a little one), broaden their horizons and kindle their imagination.

Engaged listening

The radio is a nice way to help kids feel connected to our society and culture, as well as to learn about the range of music and their own preferences and opinions. For this kind of listening, I find that BBC Radio 3 is better than Classic FM, as they tend to discuss the music, instruments and performers more and showcase more variety, but either station will provide lots of beautiful things to listen to.

Listen to the radio together and talk about the music being played – simply encourage children to tell you what they hear.

- Is it fast or slow? Notice if the pace changes too.
- Does it sound jolly or sad – or would they describe another mood?
- Is it relaxing to listen to or challenging for the ears?
- Are there lots of instruments or just one or two?
- What instruments can you hear?
- How does it make each of you feel?

This kind of discussion hones all the listening and observing skills which will later on become useful when playing music with others, or even taking graded exams or GCSE Music.

and conversational skills!

13: Musical mealtimes

Spotlight listening

See if you can concentrate on listening to just one instrument out of the group or orchestra – can you follow where the sound goes without getting distracted by the other instruments? It doesn't matter whether you manage to follow it for very long at all, and in any case not all the instruments will play continuously! But it's a fun and different way to listen sometimes and they might notice new things about the music.

More ideas:

- Concentrate on the highest parts of the music
- Listen to the lower instruments
- Follow the brass section only (trumpets, trombones etc.)
- Try to spot the drums and cymbals from time to time, if there are any
- Talk about whether it feels different to listen for just one thing, rather than absorbing the whole effect of the orchestra

Attention, aural skills (e.g. discriminating between sounds), the ability to follow a line of music – all these will be so helpful with learning pieces, playing musically and performing with other people.

and conversational skills!

The Happy Music Play Book

Story music

Programmatic music (see also 'Musical Charades' on page 74) is especially fun for active listening at mealtimes – there is a descriptive title and a story or event described by the music, so lots to listen for together as you discuss how the music represents each image. As you'll see, this is a much broader learning opportunity than just one piece of music – any of the pieces below could lead to a limitless array of conversation topics:

▸ 60

- ♪ **Saint-Saens: Carnival of the Animals** (my recommended recording: Barry Wordsworth & London Symphony Orchestra)
  Introduction and Royal March of the Lion; Hens and Roosters; Wild Donkeys; Tortoises; The Elephant; Kangaroos; Aquarium; Characters with Long Ears; The Cuckoo in the Depths of the Woods; Aviary; Pianists; Fossils; The Swan; Finale

- ♪ **Vivaldi: The Four Seasons** (Fabio Biondi & Europa Galante)
  Spring; Summer; Autumn; Winter

- ♪ **Tchaikovsky: The Seasons** (Mikhail Pletnev)
  January: At the Fireside; February: Carnival; March: Song of the Lark; April: Snowdrop; May: Starlit Nights; June: Barcarolle; July: Song of the Reaper; August: Harvest; September: The Hunt; October: Autumn Song; November: Troika; December: Christmas

- ♪ **Stravinsky: Suite from The Firebird** (Leonard Bernstein & New York Philharmonic)
  Introduction; The Firebird and its dance; The Firebird's variation; The Princesses' Round Dance; Infernal dance of King Kashchei; Lullaby; Finale

13: Musical mealtimes

♪ **Rimsky-Korsakov: Scheherazade** (Sir Thomas Beecham & Royal Philharmonic Orchestra - the heroine of the *One Thousand and One Nights* is depicted by solo violin)
The Sea and Sinbad's Ship; The Story of the Kalendar; The Young Prince and The Young Princess; Festival at Baghdad. The Sea. The Ship Breaks against a Cliff Surmounted by a Bronze Horseman

♪ **Debussy: Preludes book 1** (Krystian Zimerman)
Dancers from Delphi; Sails; The wind in the plain; Sounds and perfumes swirl in the evening air; The hills of Anacapri; Footsteps in the snow; What the West Wind saw; The girl with the flaxen hair; The interrupted serenade; The submerged cathedral; Puck's dance; Minstrels

♪ **Ravel: Mother Goose Suite / 'Ma Mère l'Oye'** (piano duet: Katia and Marielle Labeque; or orchestral: Barry Wordsworth & London Symphony Orchestra)
Sleeping Beauty; Little Tom Thumb; Empress of the Pagodas; Beauty and the Beast; The Fairy Garden

♪ **Copland: 'Billy the Kid' Suite** (Leonard Bernstein & New York Philharmonic)
Introduction: The Open Prairie; Street Scene in a Frontier Town; Mexican Dance and Finale; Prairie Night (Card Game at Night, Billy and his Sweetheart); Gun Battle; Celebration (After Billy's Capture); Billy's Death; The Open Prairie Again

You can of course go online to find the music and stories of these pieces. If you still own a CD player, though, it can be more fun to get a second-hand CD very cheaply and look at the booklet together. It will have all the details and also some interesting bits and bobs about the music and the composer.

World music

The rather broad term 'World Music' (a European and North American catch-all title) includes ethnic, indigenous, folk, traditional, neotraditional and fusion styles from around the world, as well as non-European classical styles. There is a wealth of music to listen to and this would be a wonderful thing to explore with any child, talking about other cultures and countries as you go. You could discuss:

- how it sounds different from or similar to other music they know
- whether they can recognise any instruments that sound similar to ones they know; you could look up the instruments later and see what they look like
- in what context do they think it might be played?
- whether they like the sounds?

There is endless choice of music – far too many to list – but here are a few easily available suggestions to start off with.

◯ 61

- ♪ **Guzheng Classics by Chinese Guzheng Masters** (China)
- ♪ **The Ravi Shankar Collection: Three Ragas** (India)
- ♪ The Mystery of the Bulgarian Voices: **BooCheeMish** (Bulgaria)
- ♪ Dimension Latina: **Una Dimensión De Éxitos** (Venezuela)
- ♪ **From Kuno to Kebyar: Balinese Gamelan Angklung** (Indonesia)
- ♪ Stella Chiweshe: **Ambuya!** (Zimbabwean mbira 'thumb piano' music)
- ♪ Eunice Njeri: **Natamani** (Kenya)

♪ Zuchu: **I Am Zuchu** (Kenya)

♪ Mariza: **Fado Em Mim** (Portugal)

♪ **Oniro Demeno: Greek Artists on Stavros Xarhakos Works** (Greece)

♪ Kleztory: **Nigun** (Klezmer / Eastern Europe)

♪ Los Incas: **El Condor Pasa** (Peru)

Clean-up songs

If yours are anything like mine, there's probably quite a large amount of writhing and squealing when it's time to clean their sticky hands and face, at least until they're a fair bit older. I often resort to singing silly songs and wiping in time with the beat, just to get the job done. I made up another lyric masterpiece to the tune of 'Here We Go Round the Mulberry Bush':

This little hand (face / neck / head / foot) is getting clean,
Getting clean, getting clean,
This little hand is getting clean,
Just after breakfast.

- Energetic songs work best.
- Try speeding it up as fast as you can sing
- Sing in a very high squeak or as low as your voice goes. All of these make mine laugh fit to burst. (I did warn you about leaving your dignity at the door.)
- Encourage an older child to help by choosing or singing a song for their younger sibling.

The Happy Music Play Book

Our family's favourite activities: mealtimes

Date	Name of game	Reaction
......	....	....
......	....	....
......	....	....
......	....	....
......	....	....
......	....	....
......	....	....
......	....	....
......	....	....
......	....	....
......	....	....
......	....	....
......	....	....

14 Baths and cuddles
Relaxing sound games and explorations

The evening is a really lovely time to enjoy some music together. It's very calming and cosy, and playing with sound and music is a great way to have some gentle fun without toys or screens. The bath is a particularly good place for experimental play where there's no specific outcome, since no one's going anywhere. And I'm happy with anything to stretch out that time when they're both in one place!

So here are some things to explore which I hope will contribute to a happy, calming time before bed. If you've had a long day at work, then I hope they'll help you find that precious 'quality time' together when you also want to relax.

The Happy Music Play Book

14: Baths and cuddles

Row your boat

This is an obvious one, which I'm sure most people have already thought of and is particularly excellent if you have two or more in the bath – they can row their boat in time to the song (words on page 84), maybe using a sieve or a plastic spatula as an oar. It also provides a good entry point for the following ideas.

Splash in time

This always makes me think of the chimney sweeps' song 'Step in Time' from Mary Poppins. Simple concept: sing any song and splash in time instead of clapping. Unsurprisingly, singing is even more fun when also getting water everywhere. You could explore big and little splashes, depending on the mood of the song – and how easy it is to dry your bathroom.

The room's music

Listen to the ambient sounds in the bathroom as if they were music. Really listen for the qualities of the sounds.

- How many different sounds can you count together?
- How would they describe each sound?
- High or low?
- Going up and down or staying at the same pitch?
- Repeating quickly (a car alarm outside) or a smooth continuous tone (a fan)?
- Sharp or soft in focus, nearby or far away?
- It would be particularly nice to explore the different sounds the water can make – pouring, dripping, splashing, running from the tap, rippling…

Each choose a sound that you like and talk about where you can feel it in your body, and how it makes you feel. Keep enjoying that one sound until a different one catches your ear and then move your focus to that one.

Sound in Space

(adapted from Susan Kaiser Greenland's *The Mindful Child*.[9])

Have your child listen for the sound of a bell (or triangle, xylophone, or any other nice clear sound) that you play out of their sightline. At first they can just listen and enjoy the sound.

- What does the sound remind them of?
- Where can they feel the sound in their body?
- Can they still hear it under the water? Does it sound different?

Then tell them that you're going to play it again, and they can listen really hard and see if they can hear when the sound stops. This is a wonderful calming activity – a first version of meditation! When you've had a few goes at this, you could ask them where they think the sound goes when it stops. You can also spend some time discussing how the sound keeps going even when you're not doing anything.

---

[9] Kaiser Greenland, S, *The Mindful Child*, Atria 2013.

Watery sounds

Introduce some water-themed tracks or sound effects that you can play from your phone, discuss and enjoy while splashing around. They'll suddenly have an unusually grand setting for their bath. You could try:

- rainforest
- waterfall
- whale song
- dolphins chattering
- seagulls
- waves on the beach – try lapping waves and also crashing waves.

See if they can imitate the sounds using their voice, or using the bath water (crashing waves might be a bit risky in this context!).

14: Baths and cuddles

Bathtime playlist

Below is a list of lovely pieces that take water as inspiration. Why not play one or more of them at bathtime and talk to your child about what they are hearing? You can discuss with them in what way the music sounds watery – how has the composer tried to make it sound trickling, rippling or powerful?

◉ 62

- ♪ **Debussy: Poissons d'Or (Goldfish)** for piano (my recommended recording: Arturo Benedetti Michelangeli)

- ♪ **Debussy: Reflets dans l'Eau (Reflections in the Water)** for piano (Emil Gilels)

- ♪ **Britten: 'Four Sea Interludes'** from *Peter Grimes* for orchestra (André Previn & London Symphony Orchestra)
  Dawn; Sunday Morning; Moonlight; Storm

- ♪ **Liszt: 'Au Bord d'une Source' (Beside a spring)** from *Années de Pèlerinage* for piano (Lazar Berman)

- ♪ **Liszt: 'Les jeux d'eau à la Villa d'Este' (Fountains at the Villa d'Este) from** *Années de Pèlerinage* for piano (Lazar Berman)

- ♪ **Debussy: La Mer (The Sea)** for orchestra (Valery Gergiev & London Symphony Orchestra)
  From dawn to noon on the sea; Play of the waves; Dialogue between wind and waves

- ♪ **Ravel: Ondine (the water nymph)** for piano (Martha Argerich)

- ♪ **Ravel: Jeux d'Eau (Fountains)** for piano (Martha Argerich)

- ♪ **Toru Takemitsu: I Hear the Water Dreaming** for flute and orchestra (Patrick Gallois, Sir Andrew Davis & BBC Symphony Orchestra)

- ♪ **Amy Beach: By the Still Waters** for piano (Sandra Mogensen

- ♪ **Saint-Saëns: 'Aquarium' from** *Carnival of the Animals* for orchestra (Barry Wordsorth & London Symphony Orchestra)

- ♪ **Khachaturian: 'Adagio' from** *Spartacus* – this didn't start life water-themed but it became the theme tune for the sea-faring TV series 'The Onedin Line' so I think I can get away with including it here. It is extremely beautiful and uplifting and will set you up for a relaxed evening. (Aram Khachaturian & Wiener Philharmoniker)

Echo duet

If they've finished their bath and are in their pyjamas, but you've got a bit of time before teeth and story-time, you could spend five minutes cosied up on the piano stool together, or on the sofa with one of your instruments or your piano keyboard app. Start a copying game by playing two or three notes and seeing if they can imitate you higher up or lower down the keyboard. It doesn't matter what notes they play. Ideas to try (depending on what instrument you're using) include:

- Choose one note and play it twice. Let them imitate.
- Then use the same note but play it three times.
- On the piano, choose a black note and see if they can find one too.
- Play two or three notes together.
- Play three notes in a row descending (on a piano, use white notes to make it sound like Three Blind Mice).
- Play two very short notes.
- Play a cluster with all your fingers.

They will probably also really enjoy switching roles so that you have to copy them.

The Happy Music Play Book

Love each note

Find an 'A' on the piano, keyboard or app (use the graphic here to help you) and tell your child the name of the note. With the name of the note, you could try making up a little funny song, e.g.:

- A: I'm an anteater and I like eating ants.

Encourage them to make up their own song for 'A', however silly! Keep going, creating more songs as you progress through the keys:

- B: Ball – ball – bouncing ball!
- C: A very clever cat… is sitting on a mat.
- D: Dancing dog, dancing dog – woof!
- E: E makes me smile – eeeee!
- F: Freddie is a friendly little frog.
- G: Granny is good at golf.

(If you're using a child's xylophone, the lowest bar will almost certainly be C, so start with that.)

Sing the 'song' all on the same note, while giving it as much character as you can to suit whatever words you use. This will really help them to start getting to know the sound of each individual note and distinguishing between the pitches. It's 'meaningful play' with the notes, which is exactly what helps preschoolers learn their colours, numbers and letters.

Musical conversations

This works with any instrument, or even just your voices. Take turns saying 'Hello' and letting your hand choose a note or two – any notes are fine. (It's nice if the hand is choosing rather than 'you' as it makes it more instinctive and less pressured.)

When they seem comfortable with that, see if you can respond to what the other one played. For example:

- Add an extra note on the end.
- Play the same number of notes, but using different notes.
- Play the same note they played, but very short or very long.

This is just the same as when they start to talk and we repeat back or extend what they say - 'Nana', 'Oh, you'd like some more banana?' – and is a lovely way to explore social communication. It's also a good introduction to self-expression through music. To explore further another day:

- If you're using a piano, press down the sustaining pedal for them (if they can't reach). This is the right-hand pedal and will allow the sounds to continue reverberating.
- Try varying the volume. What's the absolute quietest they can play? And even quieter? Quieter still, so it's almost nothing?

Here you are giving your child a calm space for them to explore their own creativity – this is improvisation! It is also the beginning of composing their own music.

Play to them

If you play an instrument at all, even if not very well or confidently, I really encourage you to try this if you've been putting it off – your children will think it's absolutely wonderful and it will fill them with joy to see you playing. When Laurence was very small, I used to try to squeeze in ten minutes of practice before he went to bed, by popping him in his baby chair and giving him a nightly 'concert' of something I was trying to learn. He loved it (at least for a few minutes).

All babies and children respond well to live music, but I think the effect is exaggerated when it's their own parent playing – it's so fascinating to them. I've noticed generally that they love to watch their parents doing an activity (colouring, or sticking, or building with bricks). So, dig out something easy that you used to play, set your child up on the 'listening chair' and give it a bash through.

Songs for teddies

Here are some ideas for songs that teddies can get involved in!

- ♪ 'Ten Green Bottles' with ten teddies, or however many they've got by their bed, lined up on the 'wall' and falling off one by one. ◐63
- ♪ 'Ten in the Bed'. Again, lie all the teddies in the bed with the smallest one next to the wall. Let the teddies act out the song until they're all in a pile on the floor. ◐64
- ♪ 'Teddy Bears' Picnic'. When you get to '…because they're tired little teddy bears' tuck them up in bed. ◐65

These should get some giggles, and maybe even provide an extra bedtime incentive for any reluctant sleepers. It also encourages close listening in order to react at the correct moment.

14: Baths and cuddles

The Happy Music Play Book

Our family's favourite activities: baths

Date	Name of game	Reaction
……………	………………………………	………………………………………
……………	………………………………	………………………………………
……………	………………………………	………………………………………
……………	………………………………	………………………………………
……………	………………………………	………………………………………
……………	………………………………	………………………………………
……………	………………………………	………………………………………
……………	………………………………	………………………………………
……………	………………………………	………………………………………
……………	………………………………	………………………………………
……………	………………………………	………………………………………
……………	………………………………	………………………………………
……………	………………………………	………………………………………

15 Favourite music-based books
Children's books featuring music and musicians that everyone can enjoy

There are some wonderful musical books around that would be perfect for snuggling up with before bed. I actually remember one in particular from my childhood - we had it on tape, and it has stayed with me ever since. I know the featured music like the back of my hand and the stories surrounding each piece have become part of my musical landscape. It was called 'Beethoven Lives Upstairs' and, on doing some research, I find it's from a series called *Classical Kids*. Inspired by the profound effect this had on me, I have put together a collection of highly recommended books and audio books which feature music or are about music.

Classical Kids audio books

Each composer's music is presented in historical context, told through the eyes of a fictional child who leads listeners into the composer's world. I think adults will enjoy listening to these alongside their children.

- ♪ *Beethoven Lives Upstairs*
- ♪ *Mr Bach Comes to Call*
- ♪ *Mozart's Magic Fantasy*
- ♪ *Tchaikovsky Discovers America*

The Happy Music Play Book

- ♪ *Vivaldi's Ring of Mystery*
- ♪ *Mozart's Magnificent Voyage*
- ♪ *Hallelujah Handel*
- ♪ *Gershwin's Magic Key*

The Musical Life of Gustav Mole by Michael Twinn and Kathryn Meyrick (with accompanying CD)

Gustav Mole is lucky enough to be born into a musical family, and this charming tale traces the enriching role that music plays in his life. This is the perfect introduction to musical instruments, ensembles and occasions, and a humorous and sensitive exploration of what music can bring to our lives. A favourite of all generations.

The Bear and the Piano by David Litchfield (no sound features)

One day, a bear cub finds something strange and wonderful in the forest. When he touches the keys, they make a horrible noise… This gorgeously illustrated tale of following one's dreams is sweet and touching. David Litchfield has also written 'The Bear, the Piano, the Dog and the Fiddle'.

The Story Orchestra by Jessica Courtney-Tickle (sound books)

This beautiful series brings classical music to life for children through illustrated retellings of classic works, paired with 10-second sound clips of orchestras playing from their musical scores.

- ♪ *Swan Lake by Tchaikovsky*
- ♪ *The Nutcracker by Tchaikovsky*
- ♪ *Sleeping Beauty by Tchaikovsky*
- ♪ *Carnival of the Animals by Saint-Saens*
- ♪ *Four Seasons by Vivaldi*

Poppy by Magali Le Huche (sound books)

Travel along with Poppy the dog as she discovers the sounds of music and instruments through a series of adventures. Each book has 16 buttons to push; younger kids will love listening to the sounds of the different instruments as they follow along with the (simple) story.

- ♪ *Poppy and the Orchestra*
- ♪ *Poppy and the Brass Band*
- ♪ *Poppy and Vivaldi*
- ♪ *Poppy and Mozart*

My First Classical Music Book by Genevieve Helsby and Jason Chapman (with accompanying CD)

This lively book introduces children to a variety of composers, instruments and styles of music, as well as the different settings in which they might hear music. The CD features high quality performances and your child may recognise some of the music from activities in the book you are holding. Fun for toddlers and preschoolers but will continue to interest older children with surprising facts and jokes.

Welcome to the Symphony by Carolyn Sloan and James Williamson (sound book)

"A Musical Exploration of the Orchestra Using Beethoven's Symphony No. 5". Please take your seats. The concert is about to begin! Great for toddlers and preschoolers.

Welcome to Jazz by Carolyn Sloan and Jessica Gibson (sound book)

"A Swing-Along Celebration of America's Music". Get to know the sounds and instruments of jazz, how to get in the groove, what it means to play a solo, and how singers scat. Also included are stories about how this art form started in New Orleans and how jazz changed over time as musicians like Louis Armstrong and Billie Holiday added their own ideas to it, as well a beginner's listening playlist.

Meet the Orchestra by Ann Hayes and Karmen Thompson (no sound features)

The musicians of this animal orchestra slowly gather for the evening performance… Poetic descriptions suggest the sounds of the instruments, and watercolor illustrations capture the playful essence of each musician and musical instrument.

Sergei Prokofiev's Peter and the Wolf

Prokofiev's musical fairy tale of the little boy (played by the strings of the orchestra) who, with the help of a bird (the flute), outsmarts the big, bad wolf (the French horns) is the classic introduction to music and the characters of the instruments. I have two recommendations for this story. The first is a new retelling by **Janet Schulman**, suitable for younger or more sensitive children: it follows the basic plot, but with a kinder ending for both the big bad wolf and the argumentative duck. It's a book and CD package so children can listen and look at the beautiful, Russian-style paintings (by Peter Malone) at the same time. It is also available as a digital audiobook.

My second recommendation may appeal to parents more, as it is narrated by **Sean Connery** (audio only). He takes the narration seriously and this is the sexiest version of Peter and the Wolf you will find. The traditional ending may be a little frightening for younger children. It comes on an album with *Young Person's Guide to the Orchestra* (see below) and is available as CD, mp3 or stream.

Young Person's Guide to the Orchestra Sean Connery, Antal Doráti & Royal Philharmonic Orchestra (audiobook)

An epic introduction to the symphony orchestra which children and adults have loved for 75 years. Composer Benjamin Britten wrote this piece, with narration, to show off the colours, ranges and charateristics of all the instruments. It was originally put together for a British educational film called Instruments of the Orchestra ⭕66, released in 1946, which is actually available to watch online! Sean Connery is (of course) my narrator of choice for this work.

Music (Eyewitness Books) by Neil Ardley, from Dorling Kindersley (no sound features)

If your child likes getting into the nitty-gritty of how things work, they will love this feast for the eyes. The double-page spreads contain a wealth of photos, explanations, historical asides, highlights about famous musicians, and precisely-labelled illustrations. You can discover instruments from the ancient to the modern, including such beautiful and exotic instruments as the didgeridoo, sitar and bagpipes.

16 "Can I have a song?"
Bedtime lullabies, the most important part of our day

If you choose only one activity from this whole book, make it a nightly bedtime song. This is the most precious and unchanging tradition in my household – even if I wanted to miss it one evening (which I don't) I would never be allowed to. Some of the most special moments I can remember with the boys have been those quiet times, just before they sleep, when we are each fully focused on the sound of my voice and the rising and falling melody. (During the newborn months it was definitely more hit-and-miss in terms of the aforementioned 'quiet', but on the occasions when I caught them in the right mood and at just the correct level of tiredness, it was idyllic to see them relax and watch me sing, smiling in that gentle, sleepy way that newborns have.) It is a perfect moment of stillness between the two of you with which to end each day.

I've never been a confident singer – my voice always wobbles all over the place and everything I sing turns out to be either too low or too high. But they really don't care; it's very refreshing in that sense, for me as a professional performer. It had such a wonderful effect on them both as babies (it didn't *always* stop them crying, but it often did, and definitely kept us both calmer) that it has permanently changed my relationship with my voice. What's more, I think my voice has become slightly stronger and clearer with more use.

Recorded music is also often used successfully to help babies go to sleep, but it won't have the same emotional effect as you singing to them in real life. It's *your* voice they want to hear, *your* face interacting one-on-one with them as they listen. Aside from all this, I've loved joining a world-wide and historic tradition – there's a reason why lullabies are so entrenched across all cultures and I find it immensely comforting during the sleepless newborn nights to think about the countless other parents throughout the world, throughout time, who have sung their wailing babies to sleep. If you feel nervous about singing, you could play a recording quietly and sing along – that would be beautiful too.

One problem I have consistently come up against, though, is that (despite knowing probably hundreds of songs) at the crucial moment I can never think of a single thing to sing. I got stuck for about six months just rotating between 'Frère Jacques', 'Summertime' by Gershwin, and the tune of 'Auld Lang Syne' (I still have no idea of the words). I always wished I had a list of suitable songs I knew, with the lyrics, so I could just pick one each evening when my mind went blank. So, in the hope that it will help you avoid 365 renditions a year of 'Postman Pat', I've finally made a list of uplifting, gentle, beautiful songs that are perfect for bedtime (with some space to add any of your own favourites). I find one verse is usually enough (repeated if necessary) – at least until they get old enough to start requesting more!

Choose something you enjoy singing, and don't worry about boring them if you sing the same one for a week or two while you both get to know it. I've noticed that after many performances of a particular lullaby, Laurence will start to follow the words more closely and I can see his lips making the words as I sing. This is an intensely moving experience. He starts to ask questions about the meaning of the lyrics and I leave him for the night with some new ideas to mull over. And then eventually I get some giggles myself, when he starts to reproduce each song for his teddies with varying degrees of accuracy. Remember that what's repetitive for you is comforting for little ones.

16: "Can I have a song?"

I've included the song lyrics wherever I can. For songs still in copyright (and therefore without printable lyrics) or to remind yourself of any melodies, please visit the lullaby playlist at **happymusicplaybook.com** ⏵67

Amazing Grace

*Amazing Grace, how sweet the sound
That saved a wretch like me;
I once was lost, but now am found,
Was blind but now I see.*

Baby Mine from Dumbo

Beautiful Boy by John Lennon

Beyond the Sea

Blackbird by Paul McCartney

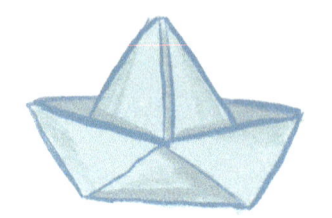

Blow the Wind Southerly

*Blow the wind southerly, southerly, southerly,
Blow the wind south for the bonny blue sea.
Blow the wind southerly, southerly, southerly,
Blow, bonny breeze, my lover to me.*

Blue Moon

Bridge Over Troubled Water by Paul Simon

Climb Every Mountain from The Sound of Music

Dance to Your Daddy

Dance to your Daddy, my little laddie,
Dance to your Daddy, my little man.
You shall have a fishy on a little dishy,
You shall have a fishy when the boat comes in.

Daisy, Daisy

Daisy, Daisy, give me your answer do,
I'm half crazy over the love of you.
It won't be a stylish marriage,
I can't afford a carriage,
But you'll look sweet upon the seat
Of a bicycle made for two.

Danny Boy

Oh, Danny boy, the pipes, the pipes are calling,
From glen to glen, and down the mountain side.
The summer's gone, and all the roses falling,
'Tis you, 'tis you must go and I must bide.

But come ye back when summer's in the meadow,
Or when the valley's hushed and white with snow,
'Tis I'll be here in sunshine or in shadow,
Oh, Danny boy, oh Danny boy, I love you so!

Edelweiss from The Sound of Music

Girl From Ipanema

The Hills Are Alive from The Sound of Music

Kum Ba Yah

Kum ba yah my Lord, kum ba yah,
Kum ba yah my Lord, kum ba yah,
Kum ba yah my Lord, kum ba yah,
Oh Lord, kum ba yah.

Someone's singing (laughing/sleepy) *Lord, kum ba yah,*
Someone's singing Lord, kum ba yah,
Someone's singing Lord, kum ba yah,
Oh Lord, kum ba yah.

Lavender's Blue

Lavender's blue, dilly, dilly
Lavender's green,
When I am king, dilly, dilly
You shall be queen.

Who told you so, dilly, dilly
Who told you so?
'Twas my own heart, dilly, dilly
That told me so.

Lord of All Hopefulness[10]

Lord of all hopefulness, Lord of all joy,
whose trust, ever childlike, no cares could destroy:
Be there at our waking, and give us, we pray,
your bliss in our hearts, Lord, at the break of the day.

Lord of all gentleness, Lord of all calm,
whose voice is contentment, whose presence is balm:
Be there at our sleeping, and give us, we pray,
your peace in our hearts, Lord, at the end of the day.

---

[10] Jan Struther (1901-53), from *Enlarged Songs of Praise*, 1931. Reproduced by permission of Oxford University Press. All rights reserved.

Lord of the Dance[11]

I danced in the morning
When the world was begun,
And I danced in the moon
And the stars and the sun,
And I came down from heaven
And I danced on the earth,
At Bethlehem
I had my birth.

Dance, then, wherever you may be,
I am the Lord of the Dance, said he,
And I'll lead you all, wherever you may be,
And I'll lead you all in the Dance, said he.

Magic Moments by Burt Bacharach

Mary, Mary, Quite Contrary

Mary, Mary, quite contrary,
How does your garden grow?
With silver bells, and cockle shells,
And pretty maids all in a row.

Moon River from Breakfast at Tiffany's

Morning Has Broken

Morning has broken like the first morning,
Blackbird has spoken like the first bird,
Praise for the singing, praise for the morning,
Praise for them springing fresh from the world.

---

[11] Sydney Carter (1915-2004) © 1963 Stainer & Bell Ltd, 23 Gruneisen Road, London N3 1LS, www.stainer.co.uk. Used by permission. All rights reserved.

My Bonnie Lies Over the Ocean

My Bonnie lies over the ocean,
My Bonnie lies over the sea,
My Bonnie lies over the ocean,
Oh, bring back my Bonnie to me.
Bring back, bring back,
Oh, bring back my Bonnie to me, to me,
Bring back, bring back,
Oh, bring back my Bonnie to me.

A Nightingale Sang in Berkeley Square

Oranges and Lemons

Oranges and lemons
Say the bells of St Clement's,
You owe me five farthings
Say the bells of St Martin's.
When will you pay me?
Say the bells of Old Bailey,
When I grow rich
Say the bells of Shoreditch.
When will that be?
Say the bells of Stepney,
I do not know
Say the great bells of Bow.

Here comes a candle
To light you to bed,
Here comes a candle
To light you to bed.

Red, Red Rose

O my Luve is like a red, red rose,
That's newly sprung in June:
O my Luve is like the melodie,
That's sweetly play'd in tune.
As fair art thou, my bonie lass,
So deep in luve am I;
And I will luve thee still, my dear,
Till a' the seas gang dry.

Rockabye Baby

Rock-a-bye, baby, in the treetop,
When the wind blows, the cradle will rock.
When the bough breaks, the cradle will fall,
And down will come baby, cradle and all.

Scarborough Fair

Are you going to Scarborough Fair?
Parsley, sage, rosemary, and thyme
Remember me to one who lives there
She once was a true love of mine.

Sing a Song o' Sixpence

Sing a song of sixpence,
A pocket full of rye,
Four and twenty blackbirds
Baked in a pie.
When the pie was opened
The birds began to sing—
Wasn't that a dainty dish
To set before the king?

Somewhere Over the Rainbow

Skye Boat Song

Speed, bonnie boat, like a bird on the wing,
Onward! the sailors cry;
Carry the lad that's born to be king
Over the sea to Skye.

Loud the winds howl, loud the waves roar,
Thunderclaps rend the air;
Baffled, our foes stand by the shore,
Follow they will not dare.

Summertime by George Gershwin

Sur le Pont d'Avignon

Sur le pont d'Avignon
On y danse, on y danse,
Sur le pont d'Avignon
On y danse tout en rond.

Swing Low, Sweet Chariot

Swing low, sweet chariot
Coming for to carry me home,
Swing low, sweet chariot
Coming for to carry me home.

16: "Can I have a song?"

Wiegenlied (Brahms' Lullaby: English lyrics)

Lullaby and good night,
You're your mother's delight,
Shining angels beside
My darling abide.
Soft and warm is your bed,
Close your eyes and rest your head.
Soft and warm is your bed,
Close your eyes and rest your head.

Yesterday by The Beatles

You Are My Sunshine

And for the month of December…

Away in a Manger

Away in a manger,
No crib for His bed,
The little Lord Jesus
Lay down His sweet head.
The stars in the bright sky
Looked down where He lay,
The little Lord Jesus
Asleep on the hay.

In the Bleak Midwinter

In the bleak midwinter,
Frosty wind made moan,
Earth stood hard as iron,
Water like a stone.
Snow had fallen,
Snow on snow, snow on snow,
In the bleak midwinter,
Long, long ago.

It Came Upon the Midnight Clear

It came upon the midnight clear, that glorious song of old,
From angels bending near the earth to touch their harps of gold.
Peace on the earth, goodwill to men, from heav'n's all gracious king,
The world in solemn stillness lay to hear the angels sing.

O Little Town of Bethlehem

O little town of Bethlehem,
How still we see thee lie.
Above thy deep and dreamless sleep,
The silent stars go by.
Yet in thy dark streets shineth
The everlasting Light.
The hopes and fears of all the years
Are met in thee tonight.

16: "Can I have a song?"

Once in Royal David's City

Once in royal David's city,
Stood a lowly cattle shed,
Where a mother laid her baby
In a manger for His bed:
Mary was that mother mild,
Jesus Christ her little child.

Silent Night

Silent night, holy night,
All is calm, all is bright,
'Round yon virgin Mother and Child,
Holy infant so tender and mild.
Sleep in heavenly peace,
Sleep in heavenly peace.

The Happy Music Play Book

Your own favourite lullabies:

....

....

....

....

....

....

....

....

....

....

....

....

....

....

....

....

Glossary
A list of musical terms for
little kids and their parents

A capella: one or more people singing alone, without accompaniment.

Accelerando: gradually getting faster.

Accompaniment: part of the music that goes with and supports the main tune. For example, a pianist may play the tune in one hand and the 'accompaniment' in the other hand, or a singer may be 'accompanied' by a band.

Audience: the people listening to a concert.

Beat: the pulse, heartbeat or unchanging speed of the music, or what you would tap your foot along to.

Bow: musicians take a bow when the audience claps after a performance, to say thank you for listening.

Brass: a group or 'family' of musical instruments made of brass, played by blowing through a mouthpiece while vibrating your lips (see page 141 for examples).

Chamber music: music played in a small group. It is called 'chamber music' because it can be performed in a small room or 'chamber'.

Choir: a group of singers all singing together.

The Happy Music Play Book

Chord: two or more notes played at the same time.

Composer: a person who makes up and writes down music.

Concerto: a piece of music written for a solo instrument accompanied by an orchestra.

Conductor: the person in charge of an orchestra or choir, who helps the musicians play or sing together.

Crescendo: getting gradually louder.

Diminuendo: getting gradually quieter.

Duet: two musicians playing together, each with their own part.

Dynamics: whether a sound is soft or loud, and everything in between.

Encore: An extra piece played at the end of a concert, if it was very good. 'The audience cheered and clapped and shouted "Encore!".'

Improvise: to make up new music on the spur of the moment.

Instrument: any object that can be used to create a musical sound.

Interval: the distance between two notes or pitches.

Legato: smooth and connected sounds.

Melody: a tune, made of a sequence of musical notes.

Music: the combination of sounds and silences, organised in order to communicate something.

Musician: anyone who plays music.

Note: a single musical sound.

Opera: a story acted out on stage, with singing instead of speaking, accompanied by music.

Orchestra: a large group of musicians playing together on instruments from the string, woodwind, brass and percussion families. An orchestra usually has between 40 and 100 musicians.

Glossary

Percussion: a group or 'family' of instruments which are played by being hit, shaken or scraped (see page 141 for examples).

Phrase: a musical sentence or statement.

Pitch: how high or low a musical note is.

Pulse: the steady beat of the music, just like a clock or your heartbeat.

Quartet: four musicians playing together, each with their own part, for example a string quartet (two violinists, one violist and one cellist).

Quintet: five musicians playing together, each with their own part.

Rallentando: gradually getting slower.

Rhythm: any pattern of sounds of different, or equal, lengths.

Scale: a pattern of musical notes going up or down in steps.

Solo: to play or sing alone, or as the main part that is accompanied.

Staccato: short, detached sounds.

Strings: a group or 'family' of instruments which are played by making strings vibrate. This can be done by plucking or stroking the strings (see page 141 for examples).

Symphony: a piece of music written for an orchestra to play.

Tempo: the speed of music.

Trio: three musicians playing together, each with their own part.

Unison: two or more instruments or voices playing the same note or the same melody at the same time.

Woodwind: a group or 'family' of instruments played by blowing and usually (but not always!) made of wood (see page 141 for examples).

Resources and further reading

Relevant research and interesting books

RESEARCH I'VE MENTIONED IN THE BOOK

(all links available on **happymusicplaybook.com**)

Chapter 1

Newborns discriminate rhythmic patterns:

István Winkler et al., "Newborn infants detect the beat in music", PNAS 106 (7): 2468-2471, 2009
https://www.pnas.org/content/106/7/2468

Babies' response to parental singing:

Takayuki Nakataa and Sandra Trehubb, "Infants' responsiveness to maternal speech and singing", Infant Behavior and Development 27 (4): 455-464, 2004
https://www.researchgate.net/publication/222742398_Infants'_responsiveness_to_maternal_speech_and_singing

Benefits of music are sustained into adulthood even if music lessons are not continued:

Erika Skoe and Nina Kraus, "A Little Goes a Long Way: How the Adult Brain Is Shaped by Musical Training in Childhood", Journal of Neuroscience 22, 2012
https://www.jneurosci.org/content/32/34/11507

Music at home has even stronger benefits than shared reading:

Kate Williams, Margaret Barrett et al., "Associations between early shared music activities in the home and later child outcomes: Findings from the Longitudinal Study of Australian Children", Early Childhood Research Quarterly 31: 113-124, 2015
https://www.uq.edu.au/news/article/2015/09/jamming-toddlers-trumps-hitting-books

Playing music improves self-esteem and independence, and decreases anxiety, depression, fatigue and feelings of isolation:

Debra Shipman, "A Prescription for Music Lessons", Federal Practitioner 33(2): 9–12, 2016
https://www.ncbi.nlm.nih.gov/pmc/articles/PMC6368928/

Synapse pruning between the ages of four and six:

Adrienne Tierney and Charles Nelson, "Brain Development and the Role of Experience in the Early Years", Zero Three 30(2): 9–13, 2009
https://www.ncbi.nlm.nih.gov/pmc/articles/PMC3722610/

Language-learning abilities in children versus adults:

D. Purves et al, "The Development of Language: A Critical Period in Humans", Neuroscience 2, 2001
https://www.ncbi.nlm.nih.gov/books/NBK11007/

Chapter 2

Flow and emotional intelligence:

M. Marin & J. Bhattacharya, "Getting into the musical zone: trait emotional intelligence and amount of practice predict flow in pianists", Frontiers in Psychology, 2013

Resources and further reading

Chapter 3
Intrinsic and Extrinsic Motivation:

Lisa Legault, "Intrinsic and Extrinsic Motivation", Encyclopedia of Personality and Individual Differences, 2016 https://doi.org/10.1007/978-3-319-28099-8_1139-1

David Epstein, *Range: How Generalists Triumph in a Specialized World* (Macmillan, 2019)

Chapter 6
Mirroring:

G Gergely and J S Watson, "The social biofeedback theory of parental affect-mirroring: the development of emotional self-awareness and self-control in infancy", International Journal of Psychoanalysis 77 (Pt 6):1181-212, 1996 https://pubmed.ncbi.nlm.nih.gov/9119582/

Chapter 7
Solfège:

In music, solfège (also called sol-fa) is a music education method used to teach aural skills, pitch and sight-reading of Western music. Syllables are assigned to the notes of the scale and enable the musician to mentally hear the pitches of a piece of music being seen or heard for the first time, then to sing them aloud. In *The Sound of Music*, solfège is the basis of the song "Do-Re-Mi" ("Doe, a Deer, a Female Deer"). Maria uses it to teach the Von Trapp children to sing. *"When you know the notes to sing, you can sing 'most anything."*

There are two types of solfège: 'movable do' and 'fixed do'. The 'movable do' system is a fundamental element of the Kodály method, used worldwide. Each syllable corresponds not to a pitch, but to a scale degree: the first degree of any major scale is always sung as "do", the second as "re", etc. By contrast, with 'fixed do' the syllables are always tied to specific pitches (e.g. "do" is always "C-natural").

Isaac Newton associated the seven solfège syllables with the seven colours of the rainbow and surmised that each colour vibrated accordingly (red has the least amount of vibration while violet vibrates the most). There are also hand signs associated with each syllable. Both colours and hand signs are used to differentiate and fix the notes in the mind of the singer.

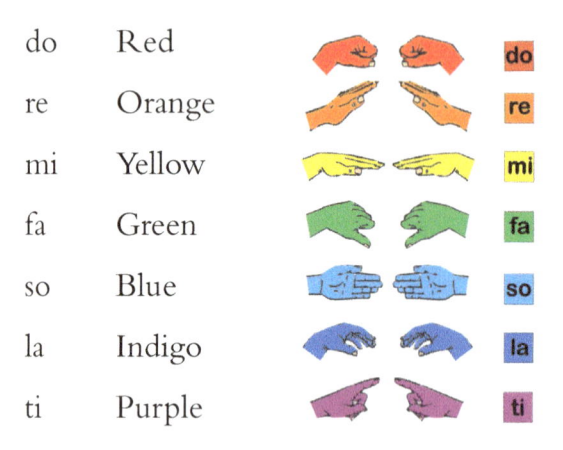

do	Red
re	Orange
mi	Yellow
fa	Green
so	Blue
la	Indigo
ti	Purple

Fixed and growth mindsets:

Carol Dweck, "Mindset: The New Psychology of Success", Robinson 2017

Resources and further reading

Chapter 8
Inhibitory control skills:

Erin Ruth Baker, Qingyang Liu and Rong Huang, "A View from the Start: A Review of Inhibitory Control Training in Early Childhood", Inhibitory Control Training - A Multidisciplinary Approach, ed. Sara Palermo and Massimo Bartoli, 2019 https://www.intechopen.com/books/inhibitory-control-training-a-multidisciplinary-approach/a-view-from-the-start-a-review-of-inhibitory-control-training-in-early-childhood

SOURCES I USED IN WRITING THE BOOK AND WHICH YOU MIGHT ENJOY TOO

Books:

Berrien Berends, P, *Whole Child / Whole Parent*, Harper Perennial 1997

Csikszentmihalyi, M, *Flow: The Psychology of Optimal Experience*, Harper Perennial Modern Classics 2008

Dowling, M, *Young Children's Personal, Social & Emotional Development*, Sage 2010

Dweck, C, *Mindset: The New Psychology of Success*, Robinson 2017

Epstein, D, *Range: How Generalists Triumph in a Specialized World*, Macmillan 2019

Gallwey, W, *The Inner Game of Tennis*, Pan Books 2015

Green, B & Gallwey, W, *The Inner Game of Music*, Pan Books 2015

James, O, *How Not to F*** Them Up*, Vermilion 2011

Kaiser Greenland, S, *The Mindful Child*, Atria 2013

Olson, M, *Musician's Yoga: A Guide to Practice, Performance, and Inspiration*, Berklee Press 2009

Pennington, J, *The Importance of Being Rhythmic*, Forgotten Books 1925 (reproduced 2017)

Perry, P, *The Book You Wish Your Parents Had Read (and Your Children Will be Glad That You Did)*, Penguin 2019

Russell, T, *Mindfulness in Motion*, Watkins 2015

Suzuki, S, *Nurtured by Love: The Classic Approach to Talent Education*, Waltraud Suzuki 1983

Urista, D, *The Moving Body in the Aural Skills Classroom*, OUP 2016

Studies:

Caldwell, K et al, "Developing Mindfulness in College Students Through Movement-Based Courses: Effects on Self-Regulatory Self-Efficacy, Mood, Stress, and Sleep Quality", *Journal of American College Health*, 2010

Juncos, D & Markman, E, "Acceptance and Commitment Therapy for the treatment of music performance anxiety", *Psychology of Music* 44 (5), 2016

Kim, S et al., "Does "tiger parenting" exist? Parenting profiles of Chinese Americans and adolescent developmental outcomes", *Asian American Journal of Psychology* 4(1), 7–18, 2013

Acknowledgements

This book would never have turned from an exciting but madly unrealistic idea into a reality without the generous help and feedback of my friends. Thank you so very much to all the following who provided my inspiration and focus group: Emma, Amanda, Emily, Caterina, Clare, Gregory, Eden, Sharon, Jonathan, Mary, Helen, Diana, Leila, Nick, Ben, Lizzie, Manon, Livia, Louise, Hannah, the Brixton/Herne Hill NCT group, Laura, Jenni, Lia, Simon, Linda, Layla, Natalie and Rachel. And, of course, to Richard, Laurence and Rafe for giving me the time to write it.

For their discussions and advice around the topic of books, children and music, thank you to Sue Hallam, Philip Ball and Rebecca Lewis-Oakes.

And finally to Cherry and Sam for believing in the idea and giving me the confidence to finish it, and to Erin and Andrew for making it look so beautiful.

Lightning Source UK Ltd.
Milton Keynes UK
UKHW050737090921
390181UK00001B/17